Developing Intermediate Care

A GUIDE FOR HEALTH AND SOCIAL SERVICES
PROFESSIONALS

JAN STEVENSON AND LINDA SPENCER

The King's Fund is an independent charitable foundation working for better health, especially in London. We carry out research, policy analysis and development activities, working on our own, in partnerships, and through grants. We are a major resource to people working in health, offering leadership and education courses; seminars and workshops; publications; information and library services; a specialist bookshop; and conference and meeting facilities.

Published by
King's Fund
11–13 Cavendish Square
London W1G 0AN
www.kingsfund.org.uk

© King's Fund 2002

Charity registration number: 207401

First published 2002

ISBN 1 85717 466 6

A CIP catalogue record for this book is available from the British Library.

Available from:

King's Fund Bookshop
11–13 Cavendish Square
London W1G 0AN
Tel: 020 7307 2591
Fax: 020 7307 2801
www.kingsfundbookshop.org.uk

Edited by Alan Dingle and Anita Reid
Cover design by Minuche Mazumdar Farrar
Figures by Peter Powell Origination and Print Limited
Typeset by Grasshopper Design Company
Printed and bound in Great Britain

Outline

Introduction   1

Part 1   The policy context   3

This part of the guide looks at the policy issues surrounding
intermediate care. It covers:

■ definitions of intermediate care
■ government policy on intermediate care
■ the trends driving the development of intermediate care.

Section 1   What is intermediate care?   5

Intermediate care is a relatively new concept. As
yet, there is no representative example showing
how it works. However, most authorities would
agree that intermediate care is a short-term
intervention to preserve the independence of
people who might otherwise face unnecessarily
prolonged hospital stays or inappropriate
admission to hospital or residential care. The care
is person-centred, focused on rehabilitation and
delivered by a combination of professional groups.

Section 2   What is prompting the development of
intermediate care?   10

Rehabilitation services for older people are under
pressure, often leading to avoidable loss of
independence for service users. In response, recent
policy documents, including the National Beds
Inquiry, the NHS Plan and the National Service
Framework for Older People, have proposed a
range of intermediate care services to build a
bridge between hospital and home, involving
closer working between health and social services.
The Government has also allocated new money,
via a range of initiatives, for the expansion of
intermediate care.

Part 2 Making the case for change 17

This part of the guide provides planners, commissioners and providers with a summary of research evidence that can be used to support plans for intermediate care and inform service developments.

Section 3 Evidence for the effectiveness of

intermediate care 19

There is a large body of research evidence to support proposals to introduce intermediate care. But this evidence has its limitations. This is partly because the evidence does not always compare like with like, and partly because there are still large gaps in our understanding of the subject.

Part 3 Making it happen 39

The remaining part of this guide offers practical guidance on how to develop intermediate care in your local care community. It offers a detailed analysis of the tasks you will need to tackle it, supported by examples of useful tools and methods. It provides a range of examples, so that readers from different agencies and professional backgrounds may choose the methods that seem most appropriate to their circumstances. This 'pick and mix' approach enables the reader to explore the potential for system changes in ways acceptable to all the stakeholders who need to be involved.

Section 4 Agreeing the future direction of intermediate

care development 43

The first step in developing intermediate care in your local community is to involve all stakeholders in creating a shared vision of the new system of services. You will first need to agree upon the values and principles upon which it will be based, and then look together at how national policy and local circumstances might affect the shape of the proposed services and making it happen. The existing services should then be mapped so that you can see where the gaps are. This will enable you to match the proposed services to the needs you have identified. An effective way to consult with stakeholders is to organise 'whole systems' events.

Section 5 Making practical plans 59

In order to deliver intermediate care effectively, you may need to redesign the local care system, either wholly or in part. Looking at information about how specific service models can contribute will be helpful. The next step is to set up the appropriate partnership arrangements with other agencies. Then you can start to draw up an action plan that specifies exactly what needs to be done, and who will do it.

Section 6 Putting intermediate care plans into practice 67

Putting your plans into practice will require strong leadership and effective management of change: you will need to engage the support of existing staff and explore new ways of working. Medical input to the new services will have to be arranged. The resulting system should be flexible enough to meet the needs of all users and to ensure continuity of care. This may involve contracting out some functions to the independent sector. You will also have to agree on a single assessment process with all stakeholders. Finally, it will be necessary to decide who will co-ordinate the intermediate care.

Section 7 Evaluation 91

The NHS and local authorities are charged with ensuring that intermediate care is suitably evaluated and that systems for evaluation are built into new intermediate care arrangements at the earliest possible stage. This section will show you how to develop a simple framework for evaluating intermediate care. The framework can also be used as a quality improvement tool if it is designed as part of a continuous quality improvement process.

Contents

Introduction   1

Part 1   The policy context   3

Section 1 What is intermediate care?   5
Some definitions of intermediate care   5
What intermediate care is not   6
Early attempts to define intermediate care   7

**Section 2 What is prompting the development of
intermediate care?**   10
Government support for intermediate care   10
    The National Beds Inquiry   11
    The NHS Plan   11
    The National Service Framework for Older People   12
The drivers of intermediate care   13
The funding of intermediate care   14

Part 2   Making the case for change   17

Section 3 Evidence for the effectiveness of intermediate care   19
The types of evidence and their limitations   19
Shortcomings of the current arrangements for rehabilitation   20
    Older people caught in the 'vicious circle'   21
Who could benefit from intermediate care?   23
    People in acute hospital beds   23
    People in long-term residential and nursing care   24
    People at home in the community   24
Which types of services can be used to deliver intermediate
care, and how effective are they?   25
    Hospital at Home   25
    Early/supported discharge schemes   26
    Rapid response   26
    Community rehabilitation   27
    Residential intermediate care   27
    Day rehabilitation   30
    The role of intermediate care in specific conditions   31
    Related services   33
What research exists on the operational aspects of
intermediate care?   34
    Assessment   34
    Team working   35
Current Government-funded research programmes   35

Part 3   Making it happen   39

Introduction to Part 3   41
    The cycle of change   41

Section 4 Agreeing the future direction of intermediate care
development   43
Agreeing shared values and principles   43
Developing a common understanding of national policy and
local circumstances   45
    Trends   46
    Uncertainties   46
    Major issues   46
Mapping existing services   46
    The basic map   47
    Filling in the detail   48
    A useful diagnostic tool   50
    Point prevalence studies   50
Matching services to needs   51
Consulting with stakeholders   53
    Case study 1 Northumberland Health Action Zone   53
    Case study 2 Mid-Hants Primary Care Trust   54
    Case study 3 Nuffield Institute for Health   55
What 'whole systems' events can achieve   56

Section 5 Making practical plans   59
Working with complexity   59
Which services to offer   60
    The balance of care approach   60
Information about individual service models   62
Partnership arrangements   63
Drawing up an action plan   64

Section 6 Putting intermediate care plans into practice   67
The success factors   67
Change management   68
    Managing change – the reality   68
    Why do we need to change?   69
    SWOT analysis   69
    Who and what can change?   70
    Force field analysis   71
    Readiness and capability   72
Securing individual behaviour change   74
The operational implications of change   74
    New ways of working   74
    The evolving role of the rehabilitation assistant   76
    Intermediate care and specialist medical assessment   76
Redesigning existing intermediate care systems   77
    Patient/user pathways   77
    Consulting clients and carers   78
    Continuity of care   78

Contracting for intermediate care with the independent sector   79

Publicising local services   81

Assessment   81

     Tools and scales   82

     Choosing an assessment tool   83

The role of the intermediate care co-ordinator   84

The context for strategic development   86

     Strategic and operational level functions   86

Section 7 Evaluation   91

Why it is important to evaluate   91

Developing an evaluation framework   92

When to establish a framework   92

Which model to use   92

Appendices   97

Bibliography   123

Index   130

Acknowledgements   132

List of figures and tables

Figure 1   Intermediate care – what is it?   8

Figure 2   The drivers of intermediate care   13

Figure 3   The vicious circle   21

Figure 4   The complex jigsaw of services providing rehabilitation   22

Figure 5   Intermediate care – the cycle of change   41

Figure 6   Rehabilitation opportunities in a complex system   47

Figure 7   London Capacity Development Team hypothetical service system   48

Figure 8   Categories of need and setting for care   52

Figure 9   Older people's services in Sheffield – layers of service provision   57

Figure 10   The balance of care model   60

Figure 11   Sample action plan   65

Figure 12   Lewin's force field model   71

Figure 13   Intermediate care services in Rotherham   81

Figure 14   Dimensions to monitor and examples of tools and measures
to use   93

Figure 15   The continuous evaluation process   95

Table 1   Point prevalence study results   24

Table 2   Model of care for people needing post-acute care for
four weeks   61

Table 3   Intermediate care and working with the independent sector   80

Table 4   Topic areas and tools/measures for evaluating
intermediate care   94

Introduction

The Government has stated its belief that intermediate care is an important approach that will help to promote independence for older people and at the same time relieve pressures on the health and social services. As a practical demonstration of support, it has committed considerable resources towards intermediate care.

Outside government, however, there is still some confusion. Because intermediate care has evolved over a number of years and in response to a number of different pressures, development has been piecemeal, and not everyone is at the same stage. However, there is already a body of evidence to suggest that intermediate care could make short-term rehabilitation services a reality and reduce pressures on hospital beds and on the long-term care budget.

This guide aims to stimulate change by providing those who will have to commission or provide intermediate care with an 'all-in-one' guide to policy and practice. We have tried to ensure that the guide has something to offer not only to people who already have a good grasp of intermediate care issues but also to those who as yet know little.

This guide will be useful for anyone who is responsible for the strategic and operational planning and development of intermediate care for older people in health, social care and housing organisations – especially intermediate care co-ordinators and senior staff working on care strategy. It will also be of interest to a range of service providers, patients' forums and older people's champions.

Part 1
The policy context

→

This part of the guide looks at the policy issues surrounding intermediate care. It covers:

■ definitions of intermediate care

■ Government policy on intermediate care

■ the trends driving the development of intermediate care.

Section 1 What is intermediate care?   5

Some definitions of intermediate care   5

What intermediate care is not   6

Early attempts to define intermediate care   7

Section 2 What is prompting the development of intermediate care?   10

Government support for intermediate care   10

The drivers of intermediate care   13

The funding of intermediate care   14

1 What is intermediate care?

Intermediate care is a relatively new concept. As yet, there is no representative example showing how it works. However, most authorities would agree that intermediate care is a short-term intervention to preserve the independence of people who might otherwise face unnecessarily prolonged hospital stays or inappropriate admission to hospital or residential care. The care is person-centred, focused on rehabilitation and delivered by a combination of professional groups.

This section will look at:
■ some definitions of intermediate care
■ what intermediate care is not
■ early attempts to define intermediate care.

Some definitions of intermediate care

The Audit Commission (2000a) has proposed a useful definition for intermediate care, which in essence states that the primary function of intermediate care is to build up people's confidence to cope once more with day-to-day activities. It serves as an extension to specialist clinical care and rehabilitation, but not as a substitute for it: quick access to specialist medical and other support when needed is vital.

Intermediate care has evolved over a number of years and in response to a variety of different pressures. One consequence of this has been that across the country a variety of different names have been given to teams and services that have broadly similar aims and objectives. Hence there is a considerable amount of confusion, among both policy makers and practitioners, about what intermediate care really is. The Government has addressed this problem by officially defining the nature and purpose of intermediate care and issuing clear criteria.

The Department of Health (2001a) set out a standard definition of intermediate care:

> To ensure a consistent approach to developing, monitoring and benchmarking services across the country. The NHS and Councils are expected to apply this definition [from January 2001] in reporting investment and activity plans for intermediate care. For these purposes intermediate care should be regarded as services that meet all the following criteria; that they:
>
> ■ are targeted at people who would otherwise face unnecessarily prolonged hospital stays or inappropriate admission to acute in-patient care, long-term residential care, or continuing NHS in-patient care
> ■ are provided on the basis of comprehensive assessment, resulting in a structured individual care plan that involves active therapy, treatment or opportunity for recovery
> ■ have a planned outcome of maximising independence and typically enabling patients/users to resume living at home
> ■ are time limited to normally no longer than six weeks, and frequently as little as one to two weeks or less
> ■ involve cross-professional working, with a single assessment framework, single professional records and shared protocols.
>
> Adapted from Department of Health (2001a). *Intermediate care.* HSC 2001/1: LAC (2001) 1. London: Department of Health.

The guidance also emphasises that:

> Intermediate care should form an integrated part of a seamless continuum of services linking health promotion, preventative services, primary care, community health services, social care, support for carers and acute hospital care. Support from these linked services remains essential for the successful development of intermediate care, to ensure that its benefits are fully realised.
>
> Department of Health (2001a), as above.

The Department of Health circular provides initial guidance on a number of other important areas:

- service models (*see* 'Which type of services can be used to deliver intermediate care?' p. 25)
- responsibility for intermediate care
- charges associated with council-arranged intermediate care services
- factors to be taken into account in planning development of services (*see* Section 5, p. 59)
- role of independent sector (*see* Section 6, p. 67)
- funding for intermediate care and community equipment services
- information that the NHS and councils will be asked to include in their investment and implementation plans for 2001–02 onwards.

What intermediate care is not

The Department of Health (2001a) also states that:

> Intermediate care should be distinguished from:
>
> - those forms of transitional care that do not involve active therapy or other interventions to maximise independence, i.e. for patients who are ready to leave acute in-patient care and are simply waiting for longer-term packages of care to be arranged
> - longer-term rehabilitation or support services
> - rehabilitation that forms part of acute hospital care ...
>
> Intermediate care services should normally be provided in community-based settings or in the patient/user's own home, but may be provided in discrete step-down facilities on acute hospital sites ...
>
> The process of assessment, appropriate patient/user selection and clear care plans are vital. It is essential to ensure close involvement of patients/users and carers in assessment and in drawing up an individual care plan that is held by the patient/user.
>
> Adapted from Department of Health (2001a). *Intermediate care.* HSC 2001/1: LAC (2001) 1. London: Department of Health.

The distinctions between what is, and what is not, intermediate care are further clarified by the following two lists, compiled by Professor Ian Philp, National Director, Older People's Services, at the Department of Health:

> Intermediate care is:
>
> ✓ patient centred, with the development of an individual care plan
> ✓ about facilitating access to acute rehabilitation and long-term care services based on need
> ✓ about active rehabilitation
> ✓ time limited, with clear entry and exit points and responsibility for managing transition
> ✓ part of a whole system approach to the delivery of health and social care to older people and related groups.

It is not:

✗ marginalising older people from mainstream services (a ghetto service)
✗ providing transitional care for older pending long-term placement (a hotel service)
✗ solely the responsibility of one professional group (a dumping service)
✗ indeterminate care (a dustbin service)
✗ a means of funding all good things for older people (a honeypot service).

Adapted from Philp, Prof. I (2000). 'Intermediate care: the evidence base in practice'. Presentation at the Royal College of Physicians/British Geriatric Society, 30 September. London: RCP.

Early attempts to define intermediate care

The King's Fund was a pioneer in conceptualising intermediate care at a time when it was not a universally accepted part of the care system. Andrea Steiner (1997) argued that intermediate care is a function of services rather than a discrete service, since many services already exist that in principle could be mobilised to meet intermediate care needs.

Steiner offered two definitions of intermediate care, first, a broader definition:

a whole set of services designed to smooth transitions between hospital and home, treat chronically or terminally ill people without recourse to hospital care, and prevent long-term institutionalisation

Steiner A (1997). 'Evidence and evaluation'. Presentation to King's Fund conference 'Care closer to home', 15 September, Ambassadors Hotel, London.

and second, a narrower definition:

that range of services designed to facilitate the transition from hospital to home, and from medical dependence to functional independence, where the objectives of care are not primarily medical, the patient's discharge destination is anticipated, and a clinical outcome of recovery (or restoration of health) is desired

Steiner (1997), as above.

This second definition was later revised to include social as well as functional independence (Steiner, 2000).

Steiner (1997) noted that the need for intermediate care could, in principle, be identified by a range of health or social service professionals outside the hospital setting, and that intermediate care could be provided in contexts other than simply 'between hospital and home'.

Lastly, she pointed out that intermediate care services border on, or overlap with, a range of existing options including shared care, community care and continuing care. These can offer a foundation on which to build intermediate care structures – but they may just as easily constitute a barrier to introducing a new paradigm of care (Steiner, 1997).

These overlaps have led many local care communities to challenge the Department of Health definition as too narrow. Developments of intermediate care before the Department of Health's circular (Department of Health, 2001a) were often designed to fill gaps in the care continuum for older people being inappropriately cared for in acute hospital beds and for whom there was little available in the form of alternative care provision, such as people who needed longer than six weeks of rehabilitation and terminally ill people wishing to return or remain at home.

The National Evaluation Team has recognised that some schemes classified as intermediate care do not fall within the definition given by the Department of Health 'but act as a crucial link in the IC chain'. They conclude that 'there will be no such thing as a typical or representative whole system of intermediate care' (personal communication, 2002).

For some years, there has also been confusion about the relationship between rehabilitation and intermediate care. Both have been described as a function of services rather than as services in their own right. The terms are often used interchangeably to describe service models based on a strong rehabilitation ethos.

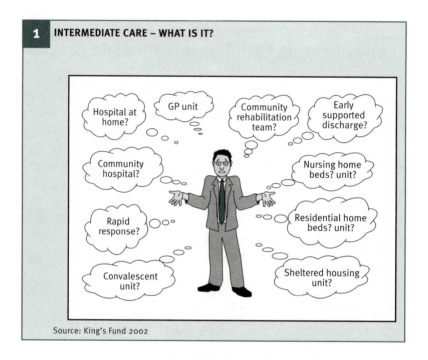

1   INTERMEDIATE CARE – WHAT IS IT?

Source: King's Fund 2002

The 'intermediate care' label has been used more widely since the Government gave priority to the development of transitional care to bridge the gap between hospital and home (Department of Health, 2000a) and included a requirement for intermediate care to be rehabilitative. Indeed, many people now regard intermediate care as a subset of rehabilitation, since it is focused more narrowly on short-term transitional care and support. (*See* 'Matching services to needs', p. 51.)

Key points from this section

- **There is no single definition of intermediate care.**
- **Intermediate care preserves independence and is person centred. It prevents unnecessarily prolonged hospital stays or inappropriate admission to hospital or residential care. It is based on comprehensive assessment and is delivered by a combination of existing services.**
- **Intermediate care does not exclude older people from mainstream services, nor is it indeterminate in duration or solely the responsibility of one service.**

Further reading

King's Fund (2000). *Rehabilitation and intermediate care for older people*. Briefing Paper 6. London: King's Fund.

Royal College of Physicians (2000). *Intermediate care: statement from the Royal College of Physicians of London*, London: RCP.

2 What is prompting the development of intermediate care?

Rehabilitation services for older people are under pressure, often leading to avoidable loss of independence for service users. In response, recent policy documents, including the National Beds Inquiry, the NHS Plan and the National Service Framework for Older People, have proposed a range of intermediate care services to build a bridge between hospital and home, involving closer working between health and social services. The Government has also allocated new money, via a range of initiatives, for the expansion of intermediate care.

This section will look at:
- **government support for intermediate care**
- **the drivers of intermediate care**
- **the funding of intermediate care.**

Government support for intermediate care

Government policy on intermediate care has developed in the wake of a series of policy and guidance papers on the theme of promoting independence through linked government initiatives. They include:

- *Better services for vulnerable people* (Department of Health, 1997a; 1998a)
- *The new NHS: modern, dependable* (Department of Health, 1997b)
- *Modernising social services* (Department of Health, 1998b)
- *Shaping the future NHS* (Department of Health, 2000b)
- The NHS Plan (Department of Health, 2000a)
- The National Service Framework for Older People (Department of Health, 2001a), which included intermediate care as its Standard Three (*see* p. 12)
- *Implementing the NHS Plan*, Department of Health 2001i).

Ministers have continued to place great emphasis on intermediate care's potential to help solve system pressures, though by early 2002 they no longer seemed to see it as the complete panacea. A further paper reviewing progress in intermediate care to date and summarising current thinking was issued in June 2002 (Department of Health, 2002a).

This latest Department of Health paper highlights the areas where action is still needed. It describes:

> The evolutionary process of locally led initiatives at the grass-roots of health and social care – small scale and often dependent on one or two committed individuals. There now exists a wide diversity of models based on local need, happenstance or opportunism.
>
> Department of Health (2002a). *Intermediate care: moving forward*. London: Department of Health.

The proliferation of schemes has led to confusion and fragmentation, and in turn to inequality of provision and access, duplication of effort, reduced cost effectiveness and lack of impact. The Department of Health sees the next phase in the development of intermediate care as one in which the growing body of evidence and evaluation will enable identification of 'service models more likely to be associated with improved clinical [sic] outcomes' (Department of Health, 2002a). It calls for local action to:

■ review existing and proposed services in the light of the principles, success factors and evidence presented in the paper
■ ensure that intermediate care services are co-ordinated and integrated with the full range of other services
■ address key issues in development
■ establish effective ways of learning from good practice and supporting professional development.

The Government has clear expectations of what the outcomes of successful intermediate care provision will be, firstly, for older people as service users, and secondly, for services and organisations. These expectations are reported in a variety of documents, some of the key statements from which are given below.

The National Beds Inquiry

The inquiry found that the health and social care systems are not fully meeting the needs of older people – as demonstrated, for example, by the shortage of community-based alternatives to hospital care, the widespread inappropriate use of hospital beds and the significant levels of delayed discharges (Department of Health, 2000b).

There was consultation on three options for the future development of care. Option Three, reproduced below, was accepted and subsequently developed as part of the NHS Plan:

Option Three: Care closer to home

Under this scenario, there would be an active policy of building up intermediate care services (i.e. services designed to prevent avoidable admissions to acute care settings and to facilitate the transition from hospital to home and from medical dependence to functional independence). There would be a major expansion of both community health and social care services. In contrast, acute hospital services would be focused on rapid assessment, stabilisation and treatment. Hospital day units and community based services would be aimed at maintaining people in their home communities in good health, preventing avoidable admissions, facilitating early discharge and active rehabilitation post-discharge and supporting a return to normal community-based living wherever possible. Over time, 'places' in community schemes might replace some acute hospital beds.

Department of Health (2000b). *Shaping the future NHS: long term planning for hospital and related services*. London: Department of Health.

The NHS Plan

The NHS Plan (Department of Health, 2000a) proposes a range of intermediate care services to build a bridge between hospital and home, and suggests where they might be offered.

The stated aims of these services are:

■ to help people recover and regain independence more quickly
■ to bring about swifter hospital discharge when people are ready to leave
■ to avoid unnecessary long-term care.

The new services will be expected to provide high-quality pre-admission and rehabilitation care to older people, thus reducing inappropriate admissions and ensuring year on year reduction in the delays to discharges of patients aged 75 years or more. Progress will be

HOW MANY PEOPLE WILL BENEFIT FROM THE REFORMS?

- 150,000 older people each year will have access to new beds or places
- 70,000 older people will benefit from rapid response and other admission prevention initiatives
- Home care will enable 50,000 more people to live independently at home
- 75,000 carers will benefit

Adapted from: Department of Health (2000a). *The NHS Plan: a plan for investment, a plan for reform*. London: Department of Health

monitored in the performance assessment framework, and an end to 'widespread bed-blocking' is expected by 2004.

The closer working arrangements between health and social services will remove outdated institutional barriers, enabling care services for older people to be improved. The NHS Plan sees intermediate care and related services as the main ways of achieving this. The new working arrangements will be jointly inspected by the Commission for Health Improvement, the Audit Commission and the Social Services Inspectorate, using the best value system.

These bodies will also assess the effect that joint working arrangements are having on:

- reducing the number of delayed discharges of older people
- reducing preventable hospital admission and re-admission of older people
- speed at which older people's needs are assessed.

As a key test of improved partnerships between health and social services, it is expected that pooled budgets and the use of other Health Act flexibilities (Department of Health, 1999a) will be the norm in arranging intermediate care services (Department of Health, 2000a).

The National Service Framework for Older People

The National Service Framework for Older People (NSF) (Department of Health, 2001b) reiterates the Government's determination to deliver real improvements for older people and their families. It expresses the themes outlined above in the form of standards, many of which focus on quality of care and rehabilitation:

Standard Three: Intermediate care

Older people will have access to a new range of intermediate care services at home or in designated care settings, to promote their independence by providing enhanced services from the NHS and councils to prevent unnecessary hospital admission and effective rehabilitation services to enable early discharge from hospital and to prevent premature or unnecessary admission to long-term care ...

Intermediate care services are expected to focus on three key points in the pathway of care:

- responding to, or averting, a crisis
- active rehabilitation following an acute hospital stay
- where long-term care is being considered.

The key to the next phase of service development is integrated and shared care, including primary and secondary health care, social care and care involving the statutory and independent sectors.

Adapted from Department of Health (2001b). National Service Framework for Older People. London: Department of Health.

Intermediate care provision must also meet the standard on person-centred care (Standard Two). In addition, there is scope for intermediate care to contribute to the care of people who have had a stroke, a fall or who are at risk of falling, and of people who have mental health problems (Standards Five, Six and Seven, respectively).

The drivers of intermediate care

Although the King's Fund work on intermediate care, reported in Section 1, drew attention as early as 1996 to the potential for intermediate care to respond to the drivers shown in Figure 2 (below), the concept did not gain official government recognition until the National Beds Inquiry (Department of Health, 2000b). Up until then, there had been a growing perception of a decline in NHS rehabilitation services.

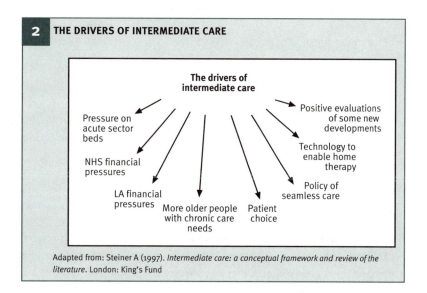

2 **THE DRIVERS OF INTERMEDIATE CARE**

The drivers of
intermediate care

Pressure on acute sector beds

Positive evaluations of some new developments

NHS financial pressures

Technology to enable home therapy

LA financial pressures

More older people with chronic care needs

Patient choice

Policy of seamless care

Adapted from: Steiner A (1997). *Intermediate care: a conceptual framework and review of the literature*. London: King's Fund

Providing rehabilitation could respond to these drivers by enabling individuals impaired by illness or injury to regain, as far as possible, control over their own lives through a mixture of clinical, therapeutic, social and environmental interventions. Policy documents tended to emphasise the need to prioritise rehabilitation services for older people (Department of Health, 1997a and 1998a).

To inform the new programme, *Developing rehabilitation opportunities for older people*, which had been set up in response to joint work by the King's Fund and the Audit Commission (Nocon and Baldwin, 1998; Robinson and Turnock, 1998; Sinclair & Dickinson, 1998), a briefing paper was produced describing the emerging policy agenda on rehabilitation for older people (Hanford *et al.*, 1999). There follows an excerpt from the policy summary given in that paper:

Promoting action

1. A lead from central government
Better services for vulnerable people (Department of Health, 1997a) and other policy papers identify rehabilitation for older people as a government priority; they also call for an end to a culture that fosters dependency. Better preventative services are also needed – ones that do not concentrate on people who already cannot cope, to the detriment of those who need less help and so get nothing.

2. New organisations and frameworks
Primary Care Groups will begin to commission programmes of care for specific populations,

such as older people; and through their commissioning, they will help to shift resources away from hospital and institutional care.

Health Improvement Programmes (HImPs) will:

■ provide a new basis for health commissioning
■ involve local authorities and Primary Care Groups, and
■ set local frameworks for action.

Joint Investment Plans (JIPs) must focus on needs of vulnerable people and require joint health–social services planning.

National Service Frameworks (NSFs) will:

■ provide standards and performance measures to reduce unfair geographical variations in care
■ focus attention on the best ways of organising care for older people.

3. Changes in the law

The 1999 Health Bill aims to extend the scope for shared funding between health and social care bodies. Rehabilitation stands to benefit greatly.

Adapted from Hanford L, Easterbrook L and Stevenson J (1999). *Rehabilitation for older people: the emerging policy agenda*. London: King's Fund.

The funding of intermediate care

Many early initiatives to provide rehabilitation or intermediate care were funded from the extra cash provided by the Government from 1997–98 onwards to help the NHS meet increased demand during the winter. Other initiatives were developed using Challenge Funding.

Some of these monies were used to fund community services to assist the rehabilitation and recuperation of older people, thus reducing the pressure on hospital beds. These services tended to stand alone, providing good rehabilitation opportunities but only for a limited number of people (Stevenson, 2000). They often struggled to attract mainstream funding, and many closed once the initial funding ceased.

At that time, the only realistic way of funding new mainstream services was to divert resources away from existing services. This is notoriously difficult to achieve.

The NHS Plan (*see* 'Government support for intermediate care', p. 10) promised significant new money for intermediate care (£900 million by 2004) and set targets for service outcomes based on the increased expenditure. This included new capital investment of around £66 million available to the NHS over two years (£33 million in 2002–03 and 2003–04) to support the development of intermediate care, and in particular an increase in bed numbers (Department of Health, 2000a).

The delays in issuing the follow-up guidance and the National Service Framework for Older People (*see* 'Government support for intermediate care', p. 10) have perpetuated the differences in how the implementation agenda is interpreted across the country. There are fears that the money may be diverted for other purposes in the NHS and local authorities (Stevenson, 2001a).

In addition to the £900 million through the NHS Plan, other, smaller pockets of new money have been allocated, with the expectation that some (or all, in some cases) would be used to support intermediate care developments. These monies include:

- The Promoting Independence partnership and prevention grants (Department of Health, 1999b)
- Supporting People grants, which will, through a new initiative, help vulnerable people to live independently in the community by providing a wide range of housing support services (Department of Health, 2001c)
- £65 million that will be provided by 2004 to integrate community equipment services (Department of Health, 2001d, 2001e)
- The Cash for Change initiative, which allocated £300 million to local authorities to free up hospital beds over the years 2001–02 and 2002–03 (Department of Health, 2001f)
- Grant for building capacity: £90.5 million is to be paid to local authorities towards expenditure incurred in 2001–02 for the provision of community care services to people who could not be discharged from hospital without them (Department of Health, 2001g, 2001h).

New money from National Insurance increases

The increases in National Insurance (NI) contributions announced in the April 2002 budget will be used to fund major new investment in health and social care. The Department of Health has outlined how this money should be used (Department of Health, 2002f) to continue the implementation of the NHS Plan.

Presenting this document to Parliament, the Secretary of State for Health said that improved care for older people remains a key goal of the reforms. He continued that the increased funds for local councils must be used to ensure that older people can leave hospital when their treatment is complete:

> The balance of services will shift, with more patients seen in primary and community settings, not just in hospitals. Social services will have resources to extend by one-third rehabilitation care for older people. Councils will be able to increase fees to stabilise the care home market and secure more care home beds. And more investment will mean more old people with the choice of care in their own homes rather than simply in care homes.
>
> Alan Milburn, Secretary of State for Health, Statement to Parliament on the next steps on reform and investment in health and social services, 18 April 2002

In order to bridge the gap, the Government has said that it will legislate to make local councils responsible for the costs of beds needlessly blocked in hospitals. At the same time, it announced increased funding for social services, at an average of 6 per cent above inflation annually for three years from 2003–04 to 2005–06.

These measures are expected to increase the provision of intermediate care by about 30 per cent by 2005–06.

League tables for social services

In May 2002, the Social Services Inspectorate published the first league tables for local authority social services (Department of Health, 2002g).

Each of England's 150 councils has been given a rating of three, two, one or zero stars, together with a judgement on how well they are delivering services for adults and children.

Councils receiving three stars will be given greater flexibility. This includes the freedom to spend social services grants and their share of the £50 million Performance Fund on any area of social services they wish, and they will also be subject to less inspection and monitoring by the Social Services Inspectorate.

Councils with zero, one and two stars will also receive a share of the Performance Fund, and will be asked to use the money to develop innovative intermediate care services. This is in addition to the £300 million already allocated to local councils to reduce delayed discharges (Department of Health, 2002h).

 Key points from this section

- **Rehabilitation services for older people are under pressure.**
- **Existing intermediate care initiatives are fragmented.**
- **The Government has promoted intermediate care through a series of policy documents, especially the National Beds Inquiry, the NHS Plan and the National Service Framework for Older People.**
- **New organisations and frameworks may also stimulate the introduction of intermediate care, for example: primary care trusts, care trusts, Health Improvement and Modernisation Plans and Annual Development Agreements (ADAs).**
- **The Government is allocating a large amount of money, under a variety of headings, for the expansion of intermediate care.**

 ## Further reading

Department of Health (2002). Implementing reimbursement around discharge from hospital (consultation document). Available at:
www.doh.gov.uk/jointunit/delayeddischarge/consultjuly02.pdf

HM Treasury (2002). *Securing our future health: taking a long-term view: final report.* (The Wanless Report). London: HM Treasury.

House of Commons Health Committee (2002). Delayed discharges. Third Report of Session 2001–02; 1. Report and proceedings of the Committee. HC 617–I.

Rose S (2001) *Intermediate care: a manager's guide.* Management Briefing. National Electronic Library for Health. Available at: www.nelh.nhs.uk/management/mantop/0117intermed.htm

Stevenson J (2001). Intermediate care. In Merry P (ed), *Wellard's NHS Handbook 2001/02.* Wadhurst: JMH Publishing.

Part 2
Making the case for change →

This part of the guide provides planners, commissioners and providers with a summary of research evidence that can be used to support plans for intermediate care and inform service developments.

Section 3 Evidence for the effectiveness of intermediate care   19

The types of evidence and their limitations   19

Shortcomings of the current arrangements for rehabilitation   20

Who could benefit from intermediate care?   23

Which types of services can be used to deliver intermediate care,
and how effective are they?   25

What research exists on the operational aspects of intermediate care?   34

Current Government-funded research programmes   35

3 Evidence for the effectiveness of intermediate care

There is a large body of research evidence to support proposals to introduce intermediate care. But this evidence has its limitations. This is partly because it does not always compare like with like, and partly because there are still large gaps in our understanding of the subject.

This section will look at:
- **the types of evidence and their limitations**
- **the shortcomings of the current arrangements for rehabilitation**
- **who could benefit from intermediate care**
- **which types of services can be used to deliver intermediate care, and how effective they are**
- **what research exists on the operational aspects of intermediate care**
- **current Government-funded research programmes.**

The types of evidence and their limitations

There is a vigorous and continuing debate between academics and between health and social care practitioners about the merits of different kinds of research methods. In seeking the evidence here, we have reviewed a wide range of literature. However, this section is not offered as a systematic literature review, but rather as a selection of evidence from various sources that we have found to be helpful. Where possible, information from published reviews has been used, supplemented by information from 'grey' (unpublished) literature and accounts from practice.

Randomised controlled trials (RCTs), which have a control group chosen at random to avoid bias, and systematic reviews, which use a systematic approach to review the literature, are considered to be the most rigorous and reliable methods. But although RCTs can be helpful when comparing the benefits of single-service models, they cannot be used to assess how the service system as a whole is functioning. The more qualitative methods lend themselves better to exploring processes and the individual experiences of users and professionals. The most important principle is to choose the method most appropriate for answering the question you wish to ask.

The evidence summarised in this section has limitations, not only in terms of how it was originally presented, but also because there are still significant gaps in our understanding of intermediate care. This is acknowledged in the National Service Framework for Older People (Department of Health, 2001b).

Sinclair and Dickinson's review of rehabilitation highlighted many of these limitations (Sinclair and Dickinson, 1998). They found:

- Important details about the components of the different interventions were often lacking.
- Different perspectives of users, carers and services were not sufficiently explored.
- Common measures of outcomes were not used, making it difficult to pool results.

Furthermore, a lack of information about the timing of the intervention, the staffing and skills mixture and many other aspects of the process make it extremely difficult to ascertain what inputs have produced the outcomes. This is a particular problem with the evidence from randomised control trials (Sinclair and Dickinson, 1998).

More recently, a review of intermediate care by the Nuffield Institute for Heath found there was a tendency to focus on regaining physical function, to take 'snapshots' during patients' journeys and to look at either a single component of care or individual model of care, usually in hospital settings, rather than at the whole of the patient's journey (Wistow *et al.*, 2002). The review notes that this approach to evaluating intermediate care ignores the potential role of prevention and health promotion in reducing and managing service pressures (Wistow *et al.*, 2002). It indicates that there is very limited evidence on whole system effects.

The evidence on cost effectiveness is complicated because it is not always clear what has been included in the costs and what has not. Where data is available, we have included it, but readers are advised to use caution when interpreting these findings.

While acknowledging these limitations, we should also put them in context. Parker *et al.* (2000), who reviewed the care options for older people after acute and during subacute illness, noted that:

> Despite considerable recent development of different forms of care for older patients, evidence about effectiveness and costs is weak. However, evidence is also weak for longer-standing care models.
>
> Parker *et al.*, 2000. Citizenship and services in older age: the strategic role of very sheltered housing. In *Housing* 21.

Shortcomings of the current arrangements for rehabilitation

In the mid-1990s, a King's Fund working paper (Robinson and Batstone, 1996) examined the shortcomings of the current system of rehabilitation and the benefits that might arise from additional investment in this area.

The authors found that there were concerns that early discharge from hospital left insufficient time for people to recover from medical and surgical interventions, with older people being especially disadvantaged. In some cases, short episodes of intensive rehabilitation in hospital were possible, but there was often insufficient follow-through in the community. The practice of providing rehabilitation opportunities in hospital environments rather than at home, or in more homely settings, was also questioned. It was unusual to find approaches to rehabilitation that entailed long-term monitoring, enabling early intervention and prevention of crises.

In addition, they found:

- Short episodes of therapy, where the recipient was signed off at the end of specific treatments, were felt to be unhelpful to people with long-term illness or disability.
- Professionals and service users both thought that too much emphasis was placed on 'minding' people with long-term illness or disability, rather than enabling them to live lives that offered greater independence, control and choice.
- There were widespread concerns about the lack of co-ordination between services and the failure to adopt care management and teamwork approaches.

The working paper reported these concerns against a background of policy statements from community care plans and joint planning documents following the NHS and Community Care Act (Department of Health, 1990) that called for new care-management arrangements to provide person-centred care – calls that had clearly not been heeded.

Older people caught in the 'vicious circle'

These perceptions were reinforced by the publication of *The coming of age: improving care services for older people*, a review of the health and social care of older people (Audit Commission, 1997). The Audit Commission found shortcomings in the way health and social services worked together to develop services that would offer alternatives to unnecessary admission to hospital, residential care or nursing homes. The report used the term 'vicious circle' (Figure 3, below) to describe how increasing hospital admissions and decreasing lengths of stay were reducing the time available for recovery and rehabilitation, and leading to growing (and unsustainable) demands on social services, especially for residential and nursing home placements. This in turn tied up resources, thus reducing the funds available for community services that could have helped to contain the increase in hospital admissions.

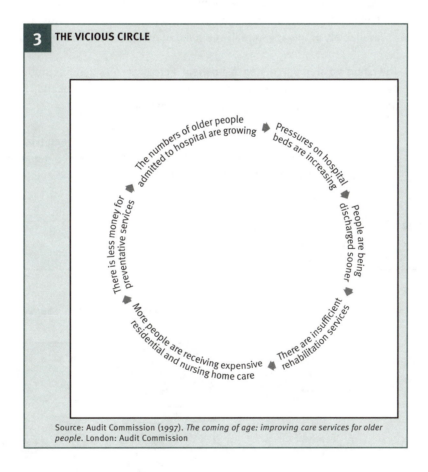

3 | **THE VICIOUS CIRCLE**

Source: Audit Commission (1997). *The coming of age: improving care services for older people*. London: Audit Commission

Recognising the key role that rehabilitation services could play in breaking this 'vicious circle', the Audit Commission undertook a comprehensive review of rehabilitation services for older people in England and Wales.

The report of this review, *The way to go home: rehabilitation and remedial services for older people* (Audit Commission, 2000a), suggested that older people who have had an illness or an accident fall into three broad groups:

1. those who will recover quickly and who do not need more than a limited amount of help with rehabilitation
2. those who will take much more time and who need a lot more help
3. those whose recovery will be limited, and who will need palliative or continuing care.

The review focused on the rehabilitation of people in the second group (whose primary condition was stroke) and identified a range of rehabilitation and intermediate care services, which it said should not exist in isolation, but as part of a whole care system. The Commission found that, in most areas, the services available reflected historical rather than planned development, producing very different patterns overall, with significant gaps.

Some areas appeared to rely entirely on hospitals to provide rehabilitation. The Audit Commission found huge variations in hospital service provision:

■ The number of beds on rehabilitation wards per head of population varied widely.
■ Some beds labelled 'rehabilitation' seem to have been used for other purposes.
■ There were big differences in the staffing and skills mixture of ostensibly similar rehabilitation services. Some supposedly 'intensive' services were found to have less therapeutic input available than general care of the elderly wards. The wards with low availability of therapy were ill-equipped to provide active rehabilitation.

The report pointed out that once a patient's medical condition has stabilised the full range of services available in hospital (whether acute or community hospital) is not always needed and intermediate care services can be used instead.

The Audit Commission concluded that a range of services is needed (Figure 4, below). In hospital, rehabilitation starts with acute care, but for those who require more time, rehabilitation may continue on specialist rehabilitation wards and in intermediate care.

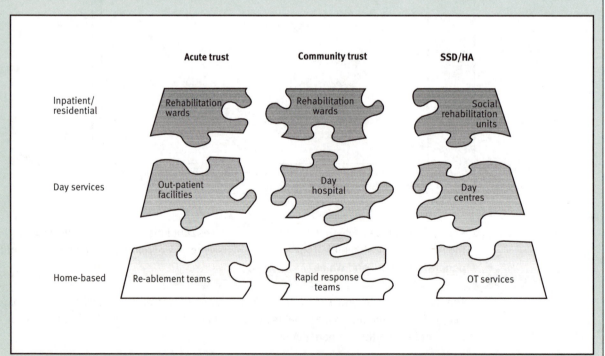

4 **THE COMPLEX JIGSAW OF SERVICES PROVIDING REHABILITATION**

Source: Audit Commission (2000a) *The way to go home: rehabilitation and remedial services for older people.* London: Audit Commission

People at home, or who have returned home, need the support of a multidisciplinary re-ablement team.

If intermediate care is regarded as a function of services (Steiner, 1997), rather than as a service in its own right, there is a growing body of evidence to inform decisions about how, where and by whom particular types of intermediate care needs can be met. These service models variously describe care:

- delivered in a range of settings
- given by groups of people who work together
- aimed at people with specific conditions
- designed to prevent inappropriate admission to hospital or premature admission to long-term residential care, or to facilitate early discharge from hospital
- designed to maximise independence.

This theme is expanded upon in Section 4 (p. 43).

Who could benefit from intermediate care?

Many people are receiving care and support in environments that are inappropriate for their needs. This is happening in:

- acute hospital beds
- long-term residential care
- the community.

A significant proportion of these people could benefit from intermediate care if the right support was available.

Furthermore, if people could be identified as being at risk of increasing dependency at an earlier stage, they could be managed more effectively, thus avoiding the necessity for crisis management. Managing this group in a different way could mean that a significant proportion will not need intermediate care or admission to the acute sector.

There is an emerging literature on the role of preventative services in minimising dependence and promoting well being (Wistow et al., 2002). However, the connections between these services are not always made, raising the possibility that intermediate care will be developed in isolation from the services to which it should relate.

A review of the literature on the effectiveness of preventative strategies found that, although there is a considerable amount of material on health, there is a lack of evidence on the social care perspective (Godfrey, 1999).

People in acute hospital beds

Recent research suggests that the proportion of patients in acute hospitals at any given time who no longer need the range of services provided by such hospitals – and could therefore be cared for in a more appropriate setting – ranges from about 20 per cent to about 40 per cent (Department of Health, 2000b; Fear, 2000; Vaughan and Withers, 2002). The patients in question were most often to be found in elderly care wards (average of 43 per cent) and were most often aged 74–85 years. However, in areas of high social deprivation, these patients were likely to be younger (Vaughan and Withers, 2002). See also the discussion of point prevalence studies in 'Mapping existing services', p. 46.

TABLE 1: POINT PREVALENCE STUDY RESULTS

On day of audit:

	Did not require acute care	Required acute care	Total
Avoidable admission	34	2	36 (33%)
Unavoidable admission	46	28	74 (67%)
Total	80 (73%)	30 (27%)	110 (100%)

Source: Balance of Care Group, unpublished internal document

Some point prevalence studies have also assessed the appropriateness of the admission, and concluded that significant numbers of older people occupying acute hospital beds did not need acute care at the time of admission. They could have been cared for in other settings, including their own homes had there been suitable services available.

Table 1 (above) gives data from a point prevalence study carried out by the Balance of Care Group that illustrates this point.

People in long-term residential and nursing care

On the basis that at least one-third of residents recorded improved Barthel scores after they were admitted, a study of 150 nursing homes concluded that 17 per cent of the people concerned no longer needed nursing care (Clinical Audit Unit, 1999). The researchers suggested that the decision to admit people to permanent nursing home care was made too soon, i.e. before rehabilitation was offered or completed. They also questioned the adequacy of the assessment process. The study concludes that 'regular national audits are needed to ensure that older people are not simply warehoused in nursing homes' (Clinical Audit Unit, 1999).

A study of residents of Scottish nursing homes found that a significant number of people with low-level needs had been placed in nursing homes because care requirements had been overemphasised (Penrice et al., 2001).

Research shows that, once people are admitted to long-term care, the provision of specialist nursing and therapy services for them is very variable (Clinical Audit Unit, 1999; Stevenson, 2001c). These services would help residents to maximise their abilities and improve their quality of life, as well as potentially preventing inappropriate admission to hospital.

People at home in the community

US researchers found that a small number of older people use a large proportion of health and social care resources. Systems were therefore introduced to monitor people with chronic health problems living in the community. Those found to be at risk of hospitalisation receive a period of intensive case management. It seems that consequently, hospital admission rates and lengths of stay have been reduced and the use of other services has declined (King's Fund, 2001a). (See also 'Assessment', p. 81.)

In the UK, there is potential for using similar approaches to relieve pressure on hospital emergency services. Recent research has found that the rate of emergency admissions for respiratory disease peaks at the same time every year, not only in London but throughout the rest of the England. Significantly, a high percentage of these admissions were older people with chronic respiratory problems (Damiani and Dixon, 2002). Primary care should be able to identify these people and improve their management, thus helping to prevent admissions. Approaches that target older people with complex conditions, such as respiratory disease, are starting to be developed, and early results are encouraging (King's Fund, 2001a).

Which types of services can be used to deliver intermediate care, and how effective are they?

Intermediate care has evolved over a number of years and in response to a range of different pressures. The result is that, across the country, a variety of different names have been given to teams and services that carry out broadly similar functions. For example, the following names were cited during a workshop on rapid response services:

- rapid response
- crisis care
- early supported discharge
- community rehabilitation teams
- community rehabilitation services
- Hospital at Home.

Moreover, the terms used do not always reflect the full range of the services provided (Spencer, 2000). In addition, the names used to describe intermediate care services also vary widely in the published studies. In an attempt to review the evidence for the effectiveness of these services systematically, we have organised this section according to the different service models involved. However, readers are warned that, in practice, two services bearing different titles can often be very similar to each other.

Where possible, the evidence given includes outcomes, financial costs and (when available) the views of users and carers. Gaps in the evidence are also highlighted (*see* 'The types of evidence and their limitations', p. 19).

Hospital at Home

Well established in many parts of the UK, Hospital at Home (HaH) services provide active treatment by health and social care professionals in a person's home, for a condition that would otherwise require acute hospital in-patient care. Hospital at Home encompasses both early discharge and admission avoidance.

Research suggests that, for people recovering from elective surgery and for older people with a medical condition, early discharge schemes may help to reduce the length of stay in acute hospital beds, providing the views of the carers are taken into account. There is some evidence that admission avoidance schemes may provide a less expensive alternative to hospital care (Shepperd and Iliffe, 2002). There is conflicting evidence on the effectiveness of HaH for people recovering from a stroke, with some suggestion of increased mortality for people treated at home at the early stages (Parker, 2002). (*See also* 'Stroke', p. 32.)

The evidence on cost effectiveness is complex. Although the cost per patient day is lower in the HaH scheme, in some cases, the longer duration of care experienced by people in such schemes compared with those conventionally discharged from hospital, is sufficient to outweigh any savings made in the in-patient costs for the HaH group (Goddard *et al.*, 1999).

A recent study (Campbell *et al.*, 2001) found that, for older people assessed as needing no more than 14 days of hospital care, HaH offers savings to health and social care agencies when compared with conventional in-patient care. However, these savings would be maintained only if the costs of expanding the service were offset by a corresponding increase in the number of patients being treated.

Users have shown high levels of satisfaction with HaH (Shepperd and Iliffe, 2002); they appreciate the more personal care and the better communication it offers, and particularly value the opportunity to stay at home (Wilson *et al.*, 2002). However, carers' experiences are more complex. Some studies found that HaH was less popular among carers (Shepperd and Iliffe, 2002), whereas other carers felt that the workload imposed by HaH was no greater than that related to hospital admission – any reduction in care duties at home is cancelled out by the necessity for hospital visiting (Wilson *et al.*, 2002).

Early/supported discharge schemes

This term covers a wide range of schemes designed to allow people to be cared for at home following a period of acute care.

A review by Steiner (2001c) found that, although early studies were not encouraging (Dunn, 1996; Bours *et al.*, 1998), the most recent research (Hyde *et al.*, 2000) concluded, with relative certainty, that early discharge:

■ reduces the length of stay in hospital for older people with hip fracture and increases the likelihood of people being able to return to their previous living arrangements (Cameron *et al.*, 2000).
■ ensures that a higher proportion of older people remain at home 6–12 months after admission, resulting in a consistent fall in admissions to long-stay care over the same period, without any apparent increases in mortality (Hyde *et al.*, 2000).

With some notable exceptions, the costs of early or supported discharge schemes seem to be lower than those of conventional care (Goddard *et al.*, 2000; Coast *et al.*, 1998).

Rapid response

Rapid response is a relatively new service that aims to provide a swift response to people's health and social care needs and simultaneously reduce pressures on the health and social care systems. Interest in the model was stimulated when the Government issued the NHS High Level Performance Indicators (Department of Health, 1999c) and the Social Services Performance Assessment Framework (Department of Health, 1999d), the findings of the National Beds Inquiry (Department of Health, 2000b) and the NHS Plan (Department of Health, 2000a).

The evaluation of the fast response service run by Rotherham Health and Social Care's community assessment treatment scheme is one of the few published studies of rapid response so far (Sanderson and Wright, 1999). The service provides short-term support (up to 72 hours) in people's homes, mainly to prevent hospital admission (about three-fifths of recipients) or to facilitate earlier discharge from hospital (about one-quarter of recipients). The researchers concluded that the service was very effective at safely diverting people away from hospital.

The cost effectiveness of the fast response service is difficult to determine, as it depends upon one's assumptions about the 'average' length of stay in hospital. However, if the 1998 NHS reference costs for relevant diagnostic related groups (DRGs) are used as cost comparators, the service is undoubtedly more cost-effective (Sanderson and Wright, 1999).

The service was extremely popular with users, carers, primary care professionals and staff based in the local accident and emergency (A&E) department or involved in hospital bed management.

One important finding was that hospital-based staff made insufficient use of the fast response service because they were not aware of its existence. This seemed to be a widespread problem: participants in a workshop on rapid response spoke of the need to 'trawl A&E Departments for referrals' and to 'work intensively with general practitioners to convince them that the service would work' (Spencer, 2000).

Community rehabilitation

The number of services claiming to provide 'community rehabilitation' has grown considerably in the last few years. However, there are enormous variations between these services. Most seem to have developed in an ad hoc manner, responding to local pressures and without the support of research evidence (Enderby and Wade, 2001). In view of the important role community rehabilitation plays in delivering intermediate care, this is an alarming trend.

The evidence to support community rehabilitation is problematic, not just because the term is poorly defined (Enderby and Wade, 2001) but also because of the potential for overlap with other models of care (Parker, 2002).

An analysis of five trials comparing the effects of rehabilitation in people's own homes with some form of hospital rehabilitation (Parker, 2002) found no significant difference in mortality or outcomes (length of stay, re-admission rates and destination at final follow-up). Nor did any clear picture emerge from cost comparisons.

The review by Parker (2002) did not investigate the experiences of users and carers. However, an evaluation of a community rehabilitation team in Portsmouth (Sander, 2000) found that users had a strong preference for home rather than hospital rehabilitation, and that the cost of care packages at referral and at discharge had fallen by an average of £96.62 per person (Sander, 2000).

Residential intermediate care

Community hospitals

Descriptive studies highlight the flexible, multipurpose role of community hospitals. However, so far, there is little evidence on clinical outcomes and cost effectiveness (Department of Health, 2002a) to suggest that community hospitals are particularly appropriate settings for intermediate care. People admitted to some community hospitals because they were said to need specialist medical cover were found to have similar levels of need to those discharged into other types of care, such as social rehabilitation (Audit Commission, 2000a).

Nurse-led units

The post-acute nursing development units set up by NHS trusts across the country are based on the concept of 'therapeutic nursing'. This means that nurses rather than doctors manage the recuperation and discharge of appropriate service users in an environment that is conducive to recovery.

However, evidence for the effectiveness of nurse-led units (NLUs) has not been encouraging. One study found there was significantly greater mortality among people in NLUs compared with those in 'normal care', although the difference virtually disappeared after 90 days (Griffiths *et al.*, 2000). Furthermore, people stayed much longer (18 days) in the NLU than in normal care – although once again this evened-out at 90 days owing to re-admissions for the control group. Another study found similar rates of mortality and dependency for the NLU and 'normal care', although the length of stay for the NLU was significantly longer at 14.3 days.

The findings on length of stay suggest that NLUs may turn out to be expensive (Steiner *et al.*, 2001a). The trial found that people on the NLU had fewer medical reviews, major or minor, and progressively less physiotherapy as their stay lengthened.

The nurses were seen to spend a great deal of time on transfers, washing, comfort, hygiene and liaison, and less time on dynamic planning for discharge: in other words, the NLU practised a traditional 'caring' model of nursing, rather than one focused on enabling and rehabilitation (Steiner, 2000). Steiner makes the important point that professionals – whether they are nurses, therapists, doctors or social workers – need support in developing the insights that will allow them to raise their expectations about the capacity of older people to recover from crises (Steiner, 2001b).

Some users and their carers described the unit as 'similar to convalescence' and 'just like the acute ward'. Others described a more positive rehabilitative experience (Wiles *et al.*, in press).

Residential rehabilitation units

Residential rehabilitation units funded by health and social care began to emerge in the early 1990s, one of which was studied at the Outlands Resource Centre in Plymouth (Younger-Ross and Lomax, 1998). Older people assessed as needing long-term care after discharge from hospital were admitted instead to Outlands for a six-week period of rehabilitation. The unit was based on a social rather than a medical model of care, and aimed to rebuild older people's confidence and physical independence so that they could manage at home (Vaughan and Lathlean, 1999). The model has since been replicated widely across the country (Ward *et al.*, 2001).

Of a group of 42 people who received rehabilitation at Outlands, only four were admitted to residential or nursing care during the subsequent five years – an estimated total saving of £456,400 (Younger-Ross and Lomax, 1998).

Although these findings are encouraging, until recently no controlled trial had been undertaken on this service model, so it is difficult to be confident about whether a different pathway of care would be more suitable to people's needs and produce similar outcomes.

Another study entitled *Buying time* compared two groups of older people discharged from a community hospital, one of which received the usual community services while the other was discharged to a short-stay residential rehabilitation unit. The study found no significant differences in terms of clinical outcomes and cost effectiveness – although the existence of the residential rehabilitation unit appeared to mean that people left hospital earlier (Trappes-Lomax *et al.*, 2002a).

The cost analysis showed that the NHS and social services costs of both groups were very similar during the year of follow-up. However, the cost of the residential rehabilitation option fell more heavily on social services, while that of the community option fell more heavily on the NHS.

Trappes-Lomax *et al.* found that users felt residential rehabilitation was well worth providing, but was difficult to do well. They differed widely in their views of the unit, but there was broad consensus about what worked and what did not. They liked the 'ordinariness' of the staff and the unit – the way it differed from hospital, encouraging independence and 'doing it for yourself'.

The things that 'could have worked better' fell into four main categories:

- Users felt isolated from each other.
- Users complained of often being bored and lonely.
- Some users would have welcomed more constructive daily activities. The rehabilitation process seemed to focus mainly on physical function – but several users would liked to have learned new things and new interests.
- Most respondents would have welcomed continuity of contact and greater support after they left the unit.
(Trappes-Lomax *et al.*, 2002b).

Another recent study (Lymbery, 2002) identified the following factors as essential to success in residential rehabilitation:

- selecting the right people for the scheme
- individualised rehabilitation programmes
- positive relationships between service users and rehabilitation assistants
- appropriate staffing
- staff commitment
- rehabilitation environment
- group dynamics
- time and timeliness
- home visits
- multidisciplinary approach
- social issues
- external factors (such as family relationships).

Nursing homes

Government has called upon the NHS and local authorities, where appropriate, to develop partnerships with the private sector to deliver intermediate care (Department of Health, 2001). A recent report from the Independent Healthcare Association (2002) describes some of the successes of such partnerships and some of the problems, emphasising that any involvement by the private sector must be at a strategic level rather than just isolated initiatives.

There is at present little published evidence on the effectiveness of intermediate care in nursing homes. Where the culture of a home has changed and staff have adopted an enabling approach that promotes independence, rather than the traditional caring model of nursing, experience from the field suggests that they can successfully rehabilitate very frail, older people (Ibbotson, 2001). However, the independent sector has had difficulty in gaining access to therapy services, which are essential to successful intermediate care. (*See the discussion on team composition in* 'The operational implications of change', p. 74.) This will clearly affect the quality of the service the nursing home sector can provide (Clinical Audit Unit, 1999).

Many of the points made in the discussion of NLUs are also applicable to nursing homes. If the independent sector is successfully to develop intermediate care, it is clear that more research and evaluation will be needed, and that effective partnerships with statutory services will need to be formed.

Sheltered housing

A relatively new setting for intermediate care, sheltered housing has the potential to offer a more homely environment than some other settings, and to give users more autonomy: characteristics that satisfy the increasing desire of older people to stay independent and their strong preferences for non-institutional housing (Fletcher *et al.*, 1999). Extra-care supported housing also has potential benefits for people with dementia, particularly in enabling them to maintain their skills and maximise their quality of life.

The potential contribution of sheltered housing was highlighted in the intermediate care guidance (Department of Health, 2001a) and more recently in *Intermediate care: moving forward* (Department of Health, 2002a).

The limited evidence on intermediate care in sheltered housing is positive. For example, the evaluation of a scheme in Derby that accommodates people unable to remain in, or return to, their own homes following illness or increasing disability found that nearly four-fifths of the users studied returned to independent living, either in their own homes or new homes, and that high levels of satisfaction were reported with the scheme (Herbert, 2002). The scheme enabled an average reduction of five hours of home care per person per week. 'Overall savings to the local authority for this group alone is in the region of £1200 per week – the equivalent of five residential care places' (Herbert, 2002).

Day rehabilitation

Day hospitals

In the past, the absence of intermediate and community-based services has often meant that day services, particularly day hospitals, are the only way of carrying out multidisciplinary assessment, rehabilitation and review outside an in-patient setting. However, day hospitals are used in many different ways, and research has shown that some have certain drawbacks that prevent them from being used to the full, such as poor co-ordination, inadequate transport arrangements and high running costs (Audit Commission, 2000a).

Comparative studies have concluded that day hospital care seems to be effective for older people who need rehabilitation, but has no clear advantage over comprehensive care (Forster *et al.*, 1999). In some areas, however, new models of day hospital assessment are being developed that attempt to respond to the changing approaches to care for older people (Black, 1998).

Day care centres

The role of day rehabilitation in a day centre was highlighted in the intermediate care guidance (Department of Health, 2001). A comparison between day hospital and day centre rehabilitation found that day centres were just as effective as day hospitals in terms of improved outcomes for users, but that costs and user satisfaction differed (Burch and Borland, 1999).

Day centre therapy was cheaper (£77.39 for a day hospital against £59.46 for a day centre). However, users felt that there was a stigma attached to a day centre service and that treatment received there was inferior to that received in a day hospital. Operational problems in the day centre were reported, such as a lack of rehabilitation space and equipment and fundamental differences between health and social services philosophies (Burch and Borland, 1999). The study does, however, show the potential contribution this model can make if such problems can be overcome.

Care at home

Home care services are numerous and very disparate, which may explain why the evidence for their effectiveness is neither extensive nor robust (Godfrey et al., 2001). The focus on home care as an alternative to institutional care has dominated the way in which services have been provided. As a result, users with particular kinds of needs have been targeted and certain types of task have been given priority. Alarmingly, for some people with high dependency, home care may make them more dependent (Godfrey et al., 2001).

More recently, however, social services have begun to accept the need for new models of home care that reflect the Government's priorities of promoting independence and supporting the development of intermediate care.

Many of these new models of home care have been developed by social services departments in partnership with other agencies. Examples include:

- home carers who work as part of an intermediate care team, such as rapid response or HaH, and who contribute the personal care element of the service. This often requires them to work closely with therapists and nursing staff to deliver the wider package of support
- the provision of more intensive support to people newly referred to home care, to minimise dependency.

The benefits of an enabling approach to home care have been known for some time (Challis et al., 1995). Kent et al. (2002) carried out a comparison between a pilot home care re-ablement service and standard home care. They found that, although the packages of care initially commissioned for users of the home care re-ablement scheme were larger, they were twice as likely as those commissioned for the matched group of service users to be decreased at first review. The pilot scheme differed considerably from the 'traditional' model of home care in both its principles and operational practice, for example, by undertaking goal setting, team meetings and reviews (Kent et al., 2002).

The role of intermediate care in specific conditions

Malnutrition

Up to 40 per cent of people admitted to hospital are malnourished (Royal College of Physicians, 2002) and many lose even more weight during their stay. Once discharged, malnourished people are likely to use more community health resources and have a 26 per cent higher rate of re-hospitalisation than those who are adequately nourished.

Malnutrition frequently goes unrecognised, both in the community and in hospitals. Screening and treatment could reduce the use of community services by malnourished people and help to prevent inappropriate hospital admissions (Rollins, 2002).

Fractured neck of femur

A study of 100 older people assessed as able to remain living independently in the community following hospital admission and rehabilitation for fractured neck of femur (Herbert *et al.*, 2000) found considerable variation between patient pathways, especially in the levels of rehabilitation inputs and the timing of therapeutic inputs. Responses seem to have been determined primarily by availability of services rather than assessment of need.

The patients who made a good recovery were generally those who had been fit and able before their hip fracture, and who also displayed confidence and determination. These findings agreed with those of previous studies on the importance of certain physical and psychological characteristics in effective recovery. However, the whole package of care, from fracture onwards, was critical in ensuring maximum restoration of function.

The cost of care for these patients was determined by the length of stay in institutional care. Acute hospital care was the most expensive, though transfers to other institutional settings could result in longer stays and hence greater overall costs. When community rehabilitation services were used, the costs were comparatively low. These services were also very effective in helping the older people regain their independence in their own domestic environment.

Stroke

Organised stroke care can bring about long-term reductions in death, dependency and the need for institutional care (Stroke Unit Trialists' Collaboration, 1997). A recent study (Kalra *et al.*, 2000) compared three different models of such care:

- a stroke unit
- a specialist stroke team that consults throughout the hospital and provides continuity of care in the hospital and community
- a specialist domiciliary team consisting of a doctor, nurse, physiotherapist, occupational therapist and speech and language therapist, with support from district nursing and social services.

Stroke units were found to be more effective than specialist stroke teams or specialist domiciliary care in reducing mortality, institutionalisation and dependence after stroke (Kalra *et al.*, 2000). This may have been because people in the stroke unit received much more therapy than those in other groups, or it could have been because of the delay that the other users experienced in receiving specialist treatment or because of the disruption caused by their transfer from hospital to home (Parker, 2002).

The key features of good stroke units have been found to be:

- co-ordinated interdisciplinary care
- involvement of family and carers
- staff specialising in stroke or rehabilitation
- education of staff, users and carers.

These same features, it has been suggested, can increase the efficacy of rehabilitation in other situations, particularly those in which several disciplines have distinctive and complementary roles to play, and in which the co-ordination of a range of inputs is required (Sinclair and Dickinson, 1998; Audit Commission, 2000a).

In the UK, up to 60 per cent of people who have had a stroke are not admitted to hospital, and many do not receive any co-ordinated rehabilitation. This is because they are judged not to require it, or because such services are not available, or for both reasons (Walker *et al.*, 1999). Occupational therapy has been found significantly to reduce disability and handicap in people with stroke who were not admitted to hospital (Walker *et al.*, 1999). This is important as evidence suggests that these types of functional improvements are associated with less need to live in institutional care and less dependence on social and health resources (Walker *et al.*, 1999; Gladman *et al.*, 1993).

Compared with day hospital physiotherapy, physiotherapy at home has been shown to be not only cost effective, but also effective in improving performance of the instrumental activities of daily living (Young and Forster, 1992).

Dementia and depression

The most frequent mental health problems among older people are dementia and depression, conditions that often go undetected (Department of Health, 2002a). Even people who have been diagnosed with mental health problems are frequently excluded from rehabilitation and intermediate care because of the common misconception that they cannot benefit from such services. This situation is recognised in *Intermediate care: moving forward* (Department of Health, 2002a), which states that:

> Services for older people should take account of the mental health needs of those they cater for, for instance by making arrangements within a 'general' intermediate care service or by developing services specifically tailored to the needs of a particular client group, e.g. people with dementia.
>
> Department of Health (2002a). *Intermediate care: moving forward.* London: Department of Health.

Good person-centred care, including the use of therapeutic approaches that enable people to regain and maintain their skills, can be critically important to the quality of life of people with dementia. For example, research has shown that people with mild and moderate dementia who fracture their hip can often return to the community if they are provided with team-based geriatric rehabilitation; one year after the fracture, significantly fewer people with moderate dementia in the geriatric rehabilitation group were in institutional care (Huusko *et al.*, 2000).

To address the problem of the widespread under-detection of depression in older people and to improve the support provided for people with dementia, intermediate care teams are developing closer links with mental health services. For example, in Portsmouth and East Hants, the community rehabilitation teams include mental health nurses, who perform a valuable role not only in identifying and treating users but also by providing support on mental health issues to other professionals in the team (King's Fund, 2001b).

Related services

Equipment services

Good equipment services are critically important for older people: 'These services have the potential to make or break the quality of life of many older or disabled people' (Audit Commission, 2000b). Equipment services are also vital to the delivery of intermediate care and rehabilitation.

The report by the Audit Commission (2000b) concluded that equipment services in England and Wales were characterised by confusion, inequality and inefficiency. A recent update of the research found some improvements, but in general services were still very poor (Audit Commission, 2002a).

The report found that ineffective commissioning lies at the heart of the problem. Services are being commissioned to match a limited budget rather than to meet need, and their effectiveness is often measured in terms of pieces of equipment rather than people (Audit Commission, 2002a). Furthermore, many services are being commissioned separately by health and social services, and there is little recognition that each benefits from spending by the other.

There was little evidence that health authorities and trusts had made the connection between the explicit NHS priorities of increasing capacity and reducing waiting times in acute specialities and the contribution that effective equipment services can make to meeting these priorities. Many acute services are struggling with the need to reduce waiting times and increase capacity. Yet, they are also experiencing an increase in admissions, with an average of 6 per cent of beds occupied by people who could be discharged if community services were available. Thus, equipment services could play a vital part in optimising capacity, preventing unnecessary hospital admission and facilitating discharge (Audit Commission, 2002a).

Voluntary sector social rehabilitation projects

A number of voluntary organisations are currently piloting schemes that have been welcomed as potentially valuable additions to the range of community services. For example, Age Concern England has set up pilot projects that involve volunteers in helping clients to achieve the personal goals they have negotiated with a paid co-ordinator. About three-quarters of all the older people starting programmes achieved some or all of their goals (Le Mesurier, 2001b). Although these projects do not meet the definition of intermediate care set out by the Department of Health (Department of Health, 2001a), they could, for example, contribute components of social rehabilitation to packages of intermediate care. (*See* 'Contracting for intermediate care with the independent sector', p. 79.)

What research exists on the operational aspects of intermediate care?

Assessment

Effective assessment leading to individual care plans is critical for the success of intermediate care. A 1993 study (Stuck *et al.*, 1993) summarised trials of comprehensive geriatric assessment (CGA) in six countries that used five different models of assessment:

- hospital-based geriatric evaluation and management (GEM) unit
- in-patient geriatric consultation service
- home assessment service (HAS)
- hospital-to-home assessment service (effectively supported discharge)
- out-patient assessment service.

Among other results, the study found that the in-patient GEM units decreased the six-month mortality rate by 35 per cent and the HAS decreased the 36-month mortality rate by 14 per cent; that the GEM, HAS and hospital-to-home assessment all improved living location; and that GEM units improved physical function at six and 12 months. There have been no similar reviews since (Steiner, 2001c).

Team working

A growing body of evidence suggests that team working can contribute substantially to improving the quality of care, the efficient use of resources and staff satisfaction and well-being.

The findings of the Health Care Team Effectiveness Project, a national study of teams working in primary, secondary and community mental health care, together with research on teams working in breast cancer care (Borrill and West, 2001a), suggest:

- Health care teams that function effectively provide higher quality patient care and introduce more innovation in patient care.
- Members of teams that work well together have relatively low stress levels.
- Particularly in primary health care, a diverse range of professional groups working together is associated with higher levels of innovation in care.
- Good quality meetings, communication and integration processes in health care teams contribute to the introduction of improved ways of delivering care.
- Clear leadership contributes to effective team processes, high quality care and innovative approaches.

Borrill C and West M (2001a). *Developing team working in health care. A guide for managers.* Aston: ACHSOR.

These findings are supported by the evidence on the effectiveness of stroke units that focuses on the role of team working (Stroke Unit Trialists' Collaboration, 1997). (*See the discussion of stroke services in* 'Stroke', p. 32.)

Current Government-funded research

The evidence base for intermediate care should expand over the next few years, as the results of current evaluations and research programmes become available. The list below is reproduced from *Intermediate care: moving forward* (Department of Health, 2002a):

Intermediate care research projects

In September 2001, the Policy Research Programme at the Department of Health, jointly with the Medical Research Council, commissioned three research projects to evaluate intermediate care services nationally (see each project). The projects are due for completion at the beginning of 2004:

1. A national evaluation of the costs of intermediate care services for older people
Professor Gillian Parker, Nuffield Community Care Studies Unit, University of Leicester
A range of research methods will be used to:
- establish the range, spread and speed of development of intermediate care services for older people nationally
- explore commissioners', practitioners' and service users' views and experiences of intermediate care
- assess the impact of intermediate care on the whole service system and on individual service users
- explore the costs of intermediate care schemes in relation to outcomes
- synthesise evidence on the costs and outcomes of different models of intermediate care and on best practice.
This evaluation will address gaps in knowledge by providing both in-depth and nationally representative information about how intermediate care policy is being implemented, what types of schemes are in place where, what outcomes they achieve across whole systems and for service users and their families, and their cost effectiveness.

2. A comparative case study and national audit of intermediate care expenditure

Professor Gerald Wistow, Nuffield Institute for Health, University of Leeds

Using a 'whole systems' perspective, the structure, process, outcomes and cost effectiveness of intermediate care for older people will be examined, focusing on impact at three levels: service system, service components and individual patient/user and caregiver. A comparative case design and a national audit of intermediate care expenditure will be used to achieve these objectives.

3. A multi-centre study of effectiveness of community hospitals in providing intermediate care for older people

Professor John Young, St Luke's Hospital, Bradford

A multi-centre evaluation to determine the health, personal experience and economic outcomes of community hospital care for older people will be conducted, using a mixed methods research design. The piece of research will provide the first comprehensive evaluation of the effectiveness of community hospital care for older people. The evaluation will make a substantial contribution to the development of an evidence-based health care policy for the location of rehabilitation care for older people. For the first time, the extent to which community hospital care can promote independence and reduce institutionalisation for this important patient group will be defined.

Department of Health (2002a). *Intermediate care: moving forward*. London: Department of Health.

See Section 7 (p. 91) for a discussion of evaluation methods.

 Key points from this section

- **There is a large and growing body of research evidence to support proposals to introduce intermediate care.**
- **This evidence has its limitations: partly because it does not always compare like with like, and partly because there are still large gaps in our understanding of the subject.**
- **Research has demonstrated that intermediate care has much to offer to people in acute hospital beds, long-term residential care and the community.**
- **A wide range of current services – in health, social care and housing – has been shown to have the potential to contribute to the delivery of intermediate care – some more so than others.**
- **There has also been research into how intermediate care can help people with specific conditions; into related services (including equipment services and voluntary sector services); and into operational aspects (including assessment and team working).**

Further reading

British Association of Parenteral and Enteral Nutrition (2000). *Guidelines for the management and detection of malnutrition*. Malnutrition Advisory Group, Standing Committee of BAPEN, November 2000. Available at: www.bapen.org.uk/screening.htm

Pencheon D (2002). Intermediate care. Appealing and logical, but still in need of evaluation. Editorial. *British Medical Journal* 324: 1347–48.

Part 3
Making it happen

The remaining part of this guide offers practical guidance on how to develop intermediate care in your local care community. It offers a detailed analysis of the tasks you will need to tackle it, supported by examples of useful tools and methods. It provides a range of examples, so that readers from different agencies and professional backgrounds may choose the methods that seem most appropriate to their circumstances. This 'pick and mix' approach enables the reader to explore the potential for system changes in ways acceptable to all the stakeholders who need to be involved.

Introduction to Part 3   41

Section 4   Agreeing the future direction of intermediate care development   43

Agreeing shared values and principles   43

Developing a common understanding of national policy and
local circumstances   45

Mapping existing services   46

Matching services to needs   51

Consulting with stakeholders   53

What 'whole systems' events can achieve   56

Section 5 Making practical plans 59

Working with complexity 59

Which services to offer 60

Information about individual service models 62

Partnership arrangements 63

Drawing up an action plan 64

Section 6 Putting intermediate care plans into practice 67

The success factors 67

Change management 68

Securing individual behaviour change 74

The operational implications of change 74

Redesigning existing intermediate care systems 77

Contracting for intermediate care with the independent sector 79

Publicity 81

Assessment 81

The role of the intermediate care co-ordinator 84

Section 7 Evaluation 91

Why it is important to evaluate 91

Developing an evaluation framework 92

When to establish a framework 92

Which model to use 92

Introduction to Part 3

The cycle of change

The diagram of the 'cycle of change' (Figure 5, below) shows what needs to be done in broad terms to redesign services so that they provide user-focused intermediate care. The following sections will work through the sequence of headings in this diagram.

The essential starting point for developing intermediate care is to bring together people from across the care system, including older people who have recently used the services, to discuss what improvements need to be made.

Your first tasks are to:

■ decide upon values and principles
■ create a shared understanding of the current care systems and care practices
■ agree on where improvements can be made.

It will be necessary to adopt 'whole systems' thinking, as your aim is to provide the right care in the right place at the right time for every individual, with seamless transitions across professional, setting and agency boundaries, as individual needs change.

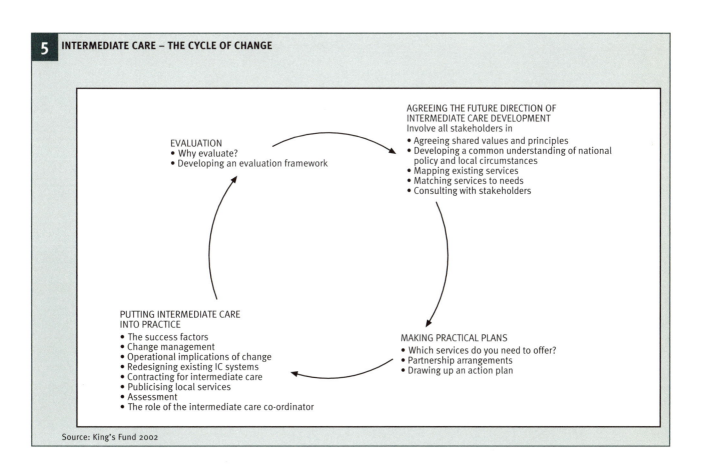

5 INTERMEDIATE CARE – THE CYCLE OF CHANGE

EVALUATION
• Why evaluate?
• Developing an evaluation framework

AGREEING THE FUTURE DIRECTION OF INTERMEDIATE CARE DEVELOPMENT
Involve all stakeholders in
• Agreeing shared values and principles
• Developing a common understanding of national policy and local circumstances
• Mapping existing services
• Matching services to needs
• Consulting with stakeholders

PUTTING INTERMEDIATE CARE INTO PRACTICE
• The success factors
• Change management
• Operational implications of change
• Redesigning existing IC systems
• Contracting for intermediate care
• Publicising local services
• Assessment
• The role of the intermediate care co-ordinator

MAKING PRACTICAL PLANS
• Which services do you need to offer?
• Partnership arrangements
• Drawing up an action plan

Source: King's Fund 2002

Once the strategic direction of travel is established, you can begin to construct a new system of care, testing out possible changes in the nature and delivery of services in accordance with your agreed vision for the future. It will be necessary to look at funding, staffing and other resource matters, and to think about what outcomes are expected from the planned changes and how these outcomes will be monitored.

The next step is commissioning or contracting for change. This will involve:

■ planning and managing change
■ developing new services
■ changing existing working practices
■ publicising new patterns of care.

Once the outcomes of changes have been monitored and evaluated, the stakeholders and you need to look at how to ensure continuous improvement in the quality of care. You will need to remind yourselves of your shared vision from time to time in order to check progress.

At various stages in the process, stakeholder agencies will each need to endorse what is being done and ensure that the necessary funding is available.

Since redesigning a care system is complex and takes time, two or more elements of the cycle of change will sometimes run in parallel, or will be repeated.

4 Agreeing the future direction of intermediate care development

The first step in developing intermediate care in your local community is to involve all stakeholders in creating a shared vision of the new system of services. You will first need to agree upon the values and principles that it will be based upon, and then look together at how national policy and local circumstances might affect the shape of the proposed services and ways of working. The existing services should then be mapped so that you can see where the gaps are. This will enable you to match the proposed services to the needs you have identified. An effective way to consult with stakeholders is to organise 'whole systems' events.

This section will look at:
■ agreeing shared values and principles
■ developing a common understanding of national policy and local circumstances
■ mapping existing services
■ matching services to needs
■ consulting with stakeholders
■ what 'whole systems' events can achieve.

Agreeing shared values and principles

The commissioning and provision of intermediate care should be based on a set of values and principles that have been agreed upon by all the stakeholders in a care community. If subsequently there is uncertainty or disagreement about particular services or settings, you can then consult these previously agreed values and principles.

The set of values given in the box overleaf was arrived at by amalgamating the lists drawn up by participants, who included older service users and their carers, in a series of 'whole systems' events run by the King's Fund in 2000, with points drawn from *Our future health* (Help the Aged Health of Older People Group, 2000) and *The carers' compass* (Banks, 1998).

SAMPLE LIST OF VALUES AND PRINCIPLES

We believe that:

1. All people should have the right of access to good quality services appropriate to their needs, regardless of gender, sexual orientation, ethnicity, age or where they live.

2. Older people should never be sent straight home from hospital or to permanent places in residential or nursing homes without proper consideration having been given to rehabilitation.

3. There should be a wide range of flexible, effective and evidence-based services available, and people should be able to move easily between them.

4. No one agency can meet all rehabilitation needs: the development of rehabilitation opportunities should be based on partnership at all levels.

5. Older people should be involved in the planning and monitoring of health and social care services; if necessary, they should be given support to enable them to do this.

6. Comprehensive and holistic assessment must be available when needed, and must be followed by care planning and regular review.

7. All rehabilitation programmes should work to client-centred goals. Clients should have written confirmation of how and by whom their agreed needs will be met.

8. All services should promote and support independence.

9. Rehabilitation should start as soon as possible with rapid interventions.

10. Rehabilitation should be provided in the setting most appropriate to the user; this must include support at home or close to home.

11. Specialist services should be easily accessible when needed, and should provide sustained input until the agreed aims have been achieved.

12. There must be effective communication and sharing of information between staff, clients and carers, and the voluntary sector, especially as people transfer between service settings.

13. Services should address the causes of physical, social and psychological problems and ill health, and promote social inclusion.

14. Staff should respect and enhance the autonomy, dignity, self-respect and individuality of clients.

15. Staff should be given appropriate training to enable them to adopt a rehabilitative approach.

16. Rehabilitation and re-ablement should be integral to the delivery of all services.

17. Good-quality information and advice presented in appropriate ways should be made readily available to older people, to enable them to exercise control over their lives and to deal with changing circumstances.

18. Independent local advocacy services should be available to support older people when key decisions have to be made and when things go wrong.

Developing a common understanding of national policy and local circumstances

The following extracts from policy documents clearly show the direction in which the Government would like to see the reshaping of intermediate care for older people proceed:

> Planning and delivering of intermediate care will require cross-agency and cross-disciplinary working across health and local government services, particularly social care ...
>
> Department of Health (2001a). *Intermediate care.* HSC 2001/1: LAC (2001) 1. London: Department of Health.

> The key to this next phase of intermediate care development is integrated and shared care, including primary and secondary healthcare, social care and involving the statutory and independent sectors.
>
> Department of Health (2001b). National Service Framework for Older People. London: Department of Health.

> The aim should be to offer users and carers a seamless service, with a range of effective and cost-effective service models.
>
> Department of Health (2001a), as above.

But how can you make sure that everyone in the local care community understands what is expected in terms of national policy and how this relates to local circumstances? One solution is to bring together a group of stakeholder representatives, including older people who use health and social care services, to discuss these topics. This approach was found to work well when incorporated into the 'whole system' planning events organised by the King's Fund in 2000 (*see* the two-day programme, p. 53). Some examples of the trends, uncertainties and major issues identified by participants in these King's Fund events are as follows:

Trends

- **person-centred care**
  rooting out ageism
- **care at home or close to home**
  relieving pressure on acute beds
  shift from hospital to community services (reflected in performance targets)
- **reducing inappropriate admission to long-term care**
  developing intermediate care/rehabilitation services
  National Beds Inquiry
- **promoting independence**
  developing intermediate care/rehabilitation services
  changing the culture from 'doing to' to 'enabling'
- **work in partnership/integrated care**
  Health Improvement and Modernisation Plans
  Joint Investment Plans
  Local Action Plans
  Annual Development Agreements
  Health Act 1999 flexibilities
  Single assessment process
- **health promotion/prevention of ill health/early diagnosis and treatment**
- **increasing money spent on health**
  the 'strings' (winter pressures, best value)

■ **social inclusion**
   Better government for older people
   Better services for vulnerable people
■ **quality/equity/appropriateness of services**

Uncertainties

■ **new money through NHS and local authorities (Standard Spending Assessment)**
   will it be spent on intermediate care or diverted to ease other pressures?
   mainstream funding for short-term funded services
   new resources, or shifting the money?
■ **impact of organisational change**
   modernisation of health and social services
   size of the change agenda
   strategic health authorities, primary care trusts, care trusts
   best value
■ **the role of housing**
■ **scarce human resources**
   changing roles/new roles
■ **decrease in the availability of long-term institutional care.**

Major issues

■ **demographic change**
   increasing life expectancy
   older old people more likely to develop chronic conditions
■ **increase in age of carers**
■ **lack of local family support**
■ **housing issues**
   care and repair
   access to equipment and home adaptations
■ **income disparity among older people**
■ **age discrimination**

Mapping existing services

By analysing how people use existing services and how they move through the system as their needs change, it is possible to create a shared local awareness of the gaps, bottlenecks and current practices affecting the ability of agencies to deliver the right care in the right place at the right time. This requires careful mapping of the services, pathways and processes within health and across health and social care, including independent sector services and leisure and recreation opportunities.

To achieve this, it is necessary to start thinking in a 'whole systems' way, as shown by the Audit Commission. In *The way to go home: rehabilitation and remedial services for older people* (Audit Commission, 2000a), the Commission developed the idea of looking at local services that provide rehabilitation to older people as 'many different pieces of a complex jigsaw that need to be fitted together' (*see* Figure 4, p. 22). After visiting 16 sites, the Commission found that, in each site, the in-patient, intermediate, day and community-based services fitted together differently, reflecting historical rather than planned development, and with significant gaps in the services available in some areas. It concluded that, although services have been developed in isolation, they should be reviewed together and should have clear links between them (Audit Commission, 2000a).

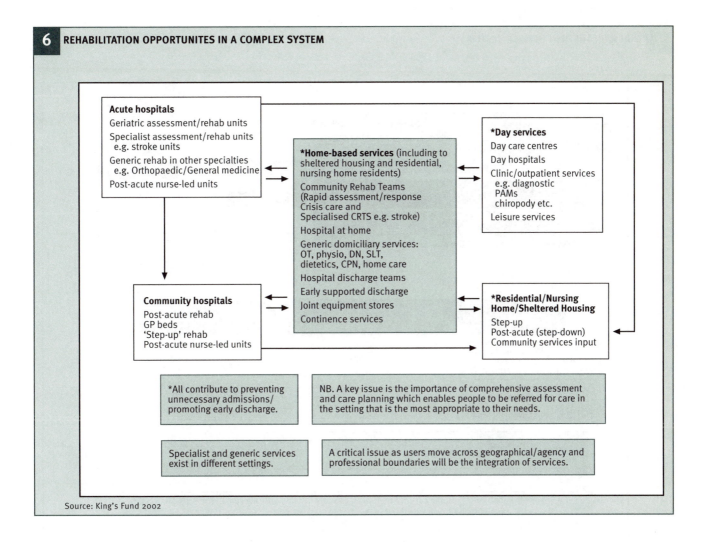

6 │ REHABILITATION OPPORTUNITES IN A COMPLEX SYSTEM

Acute hospitals
Geriatric assessment/rehab units
Specialist assessment/rehab units
  e.g. stroke units
Generic rehab in other specialties
  e.g. Orthopaedic/General medicine
Post-acute nurse-led units

*Home-based services (including to
sheltered housing and residential,
nursing home residents)
Community Rehab Teams
(Rapid assessment/response
Crisis care and
Specialised CRTS e.g. stroke)
Hospital at home
Generic domiciliary services:
OT, physio, DN, SLT,
dietetics, CPN, home care
Hospital discharge teams
Early supported discharge
Joint equipment stores
Continence services

*Day services
Day care centres
Day hospitals
Clinic/outpatient services
  e.g. diagnostic
  PAMs
  chiropody etc.
Leisure services

Community hospitals
Post-acute rehab
GP beds
'Step-up' rehab
Post-acute nurse-led units

***Residential/Nursing
Home/Sheltered Housing**
Step-up
Post-acute (step-down)
Community services input

*All contribute to preventing
unnecessary admissions/
promoting early discharge.

NB. A key issue is the importance of comprehensive assessment
and care planning which enables people to be referred for care in
the setting that is the most appropriate to their needs.

Specialist and generic services
exist in different settings.

A critical issue as users move across geographical/agency and
professional boundaries will be the integration of services.

Source: King's Fund 2002

A similar approach was taken by the King's Fund Rehabilitation Programme, which proposed a
simpler picture of the ideal service system (Figure 6, above), including sample client pathways
and showing the kinds of services that should be offering care with a rehabilitative approach.

Both these approaches, as shown in Figures 4 (p. 22) and 6 (above), offer a good starting
point for local debate. How do these pictures fit the service reality in your area?

The basic map

Using a 'whole systems' approach, construct a basic map of where older people's needs are –
or could be – met in the local system of services. Include details of all services and settings
that offer care and support, even though their relevance to rehabilitation and intermediate
care may appear tenuous. Effective care packages are those that are tailored to each
individual's needs and adopt a holistic approach – which means that those who put the
packages together need to be aware of the potential contributions of a wide range of services,
leisure opportunities, sources of advice, and so on.

People from different agencies and older people themselves should be involved in this
exercise, as each will bring a different perspective and different local knowledge to the task.

As part of its work to support the longer-term development of older people's services, the
London Capacity Development Team drew a map of a hypothetical service system (Figure 7,
overleaf).

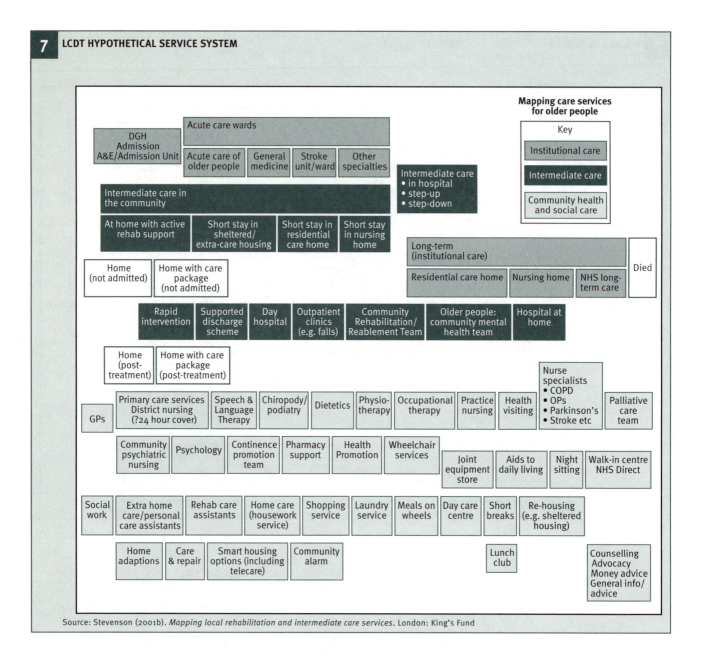

7 LCDT HYPOTHETICAL SERVICE SYSTEM

Source: Stevenson (2001b). *Mapping local rehabilitation and intermediate care services.* London: King's Fund

Filling in the detail

Once the outline mapping exercise has been completed, seek out other local information to help you understand how well or badly the system is operating. This additional information can be plotted on to transparent pages, which can then be overlaid on to the basic service map, so helping you to understand how the system fits together. For example, consider the following:

Gaps

Check to see if there are any gaps in the system. Comparing this map with the one in Figure 7 (above) may help spot the gaps. Questions to ask include:

■ Are older people with specific rehabilitation or intermediate care needs either being given no support at all, or being given it in an inappropriate manner?

■ For example, is there a choice of intermediate care settings, or are older people simply moved to the one place locally that offers intermediate care?

■ Are services labelled 'rehabilitation' or 'intermediate care' in fact able to provide
  such care?

Check staffing levels, training, access to therapists, etc. (*See* 'Matching services to needs',
p. 51).

Access and equity

Who is using the system?

■ Are people from certain groups using the system less than you might expect from their
  representation in the local population?
■ Are local ethnic groups under-represented?

Identify where people gain access to the system.

■ Who are the referrers?
■ Do the sources or patterns of referral differ in different parts of the system?
■ Are any of the referrers acting as 'gatekeepers'?
■ Are referrals appropriate?

(*See the discussion on specific conditions in* 'Which types of services can be used to deliver
intermediate care?', p. 25)

Check the eligibility criteria used by services.

■ Are there explicit exclusions, such as people with dementia?
■ Are the needs of those who are excluded catered for elsewhere in the system?
■ Does everyone who needs to know have this information?
■ If there are no clear criteria, they need to be developed.

Bottlenecks

Look for bottlenecks in service provision.

■ Are there any points of access that have waiting lists, or that are seen as bottlenecks?
■ If so, what effect do they have on the system as a whole? For example, are there long waits
  for community equipment services to support hospital discharge?
■ Check whether any of these bottlenecks affect the ability of the local community to meet
  government performance targets. (*See* 'Point prevalence studies', overleaf.)

Moving through the system

■ Are there agreed pathways for users through the care system, based on assessed need?
■ Does everyone who needs to know have this information?
■ Are there agreed protocols for transfers between different parts of the system? If not, these
  will need to be developed.
■ Are there cross-boundary issues for some service users and are these explicitly dealt with
  in eligibility criteria and transfer protocols? (If not, they too will need to be addressed.)

Impact of local policies

■ Are there local policies that affect patient care and pathways? For example, local authority
  charging policies can deter people from using some services.

The end result

The level of sophistication you can achieve in this task depends upon:

- the amount of time and resources you can give to the work
- how comprehensive are the information systems of local agencies, and how easy it is to retrieve the data.

The fuller the picture obtained, the easier it will be for you and your local planning partners to construct a vision of the future pattern of care that might best meet local needs. It will also make it easier to predict the effects of your proposed changes in advance and to test them after implementation (Stevenson, 2001b).

A useful diagnostic tool

Another way of gathering information about local services and identifying the potential for change is to use the Initial Diagnostic Tool devised by the NHS Executive and Social Services Inspectorate South West Regional Office (NHS Executive South West/SSI South West Regional Office, 2001a). This is a checklist of issues that the NHS, social services, housing departments and other agencies might need to consider in developing a new range of intermediate care services (Appendix 1). Its aim is 'to explore ways in which capacity can be increased across the care system by looking at the appropriate use of data, the effectiveness/timeliness of systems and processes and the appropriate service response to needs.' @

> @
> The Initial Diagnostic Tool can be downloaded at: www.doh.gov.uk/swo/olderpeopleservices.htm

Point prevalence studies

Some aspects of current services, such as the level of avoidable admissions and the reasons for delayed discharges, may merit closer analysis.

The largest group of potential users of intermediate care are older people who could be supported at home or closer to home, either to avoid unnecessary hospital admission or to expedite their discharge once they no longer need acute hospital care.

Local stakeholders often disagree over the numbers of people falling into either of these categories; and the ability of staff outside the acute hospital sector to provide appropriate care for such people is frequently disputed by staff within that sector. In practice, needs are not always recognised until viable alternatives to current services are offered (Vaughan and Lathlean, 1999). Even then, a considerable period of time and a certain amount of information sharing and training are needed before acute sector staff begin to make appropriate referrals of in-patients who might benefit from intermediate care.

To create a shared local understanding of how many people might fall into this category, point prevalence studies have been undertaken in a large number of hospitals.

The usual method is carry out a survey over a short space of time of most or all medical in-patients aged 75 years and over. The focus is on identifying people whose admission was avoidable or who are medically stable but whose discharge is delayed for a variety of reasons. To ensure that the results are acceptable to all participants, the process followed must be transparent and agreed in advance. To avoid local bias, the review is often done by independent experts who are knowledgeable about the potential for keeping people out of acute care or for delivering post-acute care in different settings using different models. One method often used is the appropriateness evaluation protocol (AEP).

Point prevalence studies can increase local awareness of the potential for caring for people in new ways and of the need to develop new care pathways and models of care. Planners and commissioners can then discuss reshaping the local care system in the confidence that key stakeholders will share their vision and work with them to bring about change. (*See* evidence from point prevalence studies in 'Who could benefit from intermediate care?', p. 23.)

Matching services to needs

When planners and commissioners begin to explore how care is delivered locally, they usually think in terms of specific services or settings. It is rare to find people who start from a needs-led perspective, looking at where and by whom care needs – and in particular, rehabilitation needs – are currently being met.

Even when commissioners are planning new services, they are often unclear about which needs and whose needs these services are intended to meet:

> A number of new initiatives have been explored ... yet there is little agreement about what is meant by intermediate or transitional care; the needs and size of the potential target group who may benefit; the objectives of the care alternatives; and the efficacy of the services.
>
> Steiner A (1997). *Intermediate care: a conceptual framework and review of the literature.* London: King's Fund.

Typical examples were the projects set up quickly to use money allocated for easing winter pressures on hospital care. Many of these were short-term 'quick fixes' to ease some of the pressures on the care system, with little thought given to how their impact would be assessed.

It is therefore more useful to start by looking at where specific rehabilitation needs are actually being met, rather than by simply recording services that are labelled 'rehabilitation' or 'intermediate care'. For example, planning partners in Sheffield wanted to review existing opportunities for rehabilitation and intermediate care using a whole systems approach (Enderby and Stevenson, 2000). They aimed to identify both the gaps in the system and the points at which intermediate care could be offered in a setting more appropriate to a person's needs, rather than adopting the more common approach of fitting people into the services provided.

During the planning process, the partners realised that when they focused on existing local services, their thinking was constrained, so they decided instead to consider people's needs and where these might best be met. They defined eight broad categories of care needs among people with disabling conditions (*see* box below).

THE EIGHT CATEGORIES OF CARE NEEDS

1. Person needs prevention/maintenance programme
2. Person needs active convalescence
3. Person needs slow-stream rehabilitation
4. Person needs regular rehabilitation
5. Person needs intensive rehabilitation
6. Person needs specific treatment for individual acute disabling condition
7. Person needs medical care and rehabilitation
8. Person needs rehabilitation for complex, profound disabling condition

The focus is on meeting rehabilitation needs, rather than intermediate care needs, which must according to the Department of Health definition, include a rehabilitation component. People's needs change over time, and many will need rehabilitation care over longer periods, or intermittently, to maintain or improve their quality of life.

More detailed descriptions of the aims of the care programme for each group, the services and settings that might be involved, the status of the user and the inclusion and exclusion criteria are given in Appendix 2, p. 103.

In Figure 8 (below), the eight categories of need are arranged in order of the expected number of users in each, with the largest category, 'prevention and maintenance', at the top. The places where people's rehabilitation needs might be met are listed along the top. By looking at if and where these needs are currently being met, and where they might best be met if alternative services existed (or pathways of care were managed differently), it is possible to identify where there is potential for change.

In many places, care is currently provided higher 'upstream' in the system than is appropriate because of the lack of investment in alternative services. If the locally agreed values and principles (*See* 'Sample list of values and principles', p. 44) include an aspiration to deliver the right care in the right place at the right time, then the system may need reshaping to deliver care at home or closer to home.

Do not continue with current practices without re-examining them in the light of new policies and values. Above all, aim for shared ownership of a vision – and of the challenges to be met in realising it.

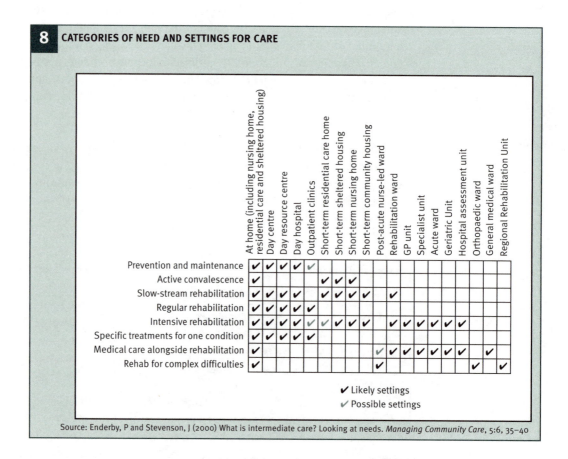

8 CATEGORIES OF NEED AND SETTINGS FOR CARE

	At home (including nursing home, residential care and sheltered housing)	Day centre	Day resource centre	Day hospital	Outpatient clinics	Short-term residential care home	Short-term sheltered housing	Short-term nursing home	Short-term community housing	Post-acute nurse-led ward	Rehabilitation ward	GP unit	Specialist unit	Acute ward	Geriatric Unit	Hospital assessment unit	Orthopaedic ward	General medical ward	Regional Rehabilitation Unit
Prevention and maintenance	✔	✔	✔	✔	(✔)														
Active convalescence	✔					✔	✔	✔											
Slow-stream rehabilitation	✔	✔	✔	✔		✔	✔	✔	✔		✔								
Regular rehabilitation	✔	✔	✔	✔	✔														
Intensive rehabilitation	✔	✔	✔	✔	(✔)	(✔)	✔	✔	✔			✔	✔	✔	✔	✔	✔		
Specific treatments for one condition	✔	✔	✔	✔	✔														
Medical care alongside rehabilitation	✔									(✔)	✔	✔	✔	✔	✔	✔		✔	
Rehab for complex difficulties	✔										✔							✔	✔

✔ Likely settings
✔ Possible settings

Source: Enderby, P and Stevenson, J (2000) What is intermediate care? Looking at needs. *Managing Community Care*, 5:6, 35–40

Consulting with stakeholders

Looking at needs can help to open up the theme of delivering care in different ways and in different places, but it does not work for all stakeholders. A range of different workshop formats may be needed to engage people in discussions about new ways of working.

The two-day 'whole system' events run by the King's Fund in nine care communities were very successful in eliciting the views of older service users. Participants were led through a process that encouraged them to comment on existing patterns of care and to consider changes that might meet older people's needs in ways that are more acceptable. A sample programme is shown in the box below.

TWO-DAY PROGRAMME FOR DEVELOPING REHABILITATION OPPORTUNITIES FOR OLDER PEOPLE

Day one
- workshop overview and procedures (15 minutes)
- mapping services (75 minutes)
- present trends/what's good (90 minutes)
- values/principles (30 minutes)
- focus on the future (100 minutes)

Day two
- plan for the day (10 minutes)
- identifying common ground (50 minutes)
- negotiate priorities (60 minutes)
- action planning (90 minutes)
- feedback (30 minutes)
- next steps (40 minutes)

Adapted from Northumberland Health Action Zone Person Centred Care Programme (2000). *Show me the way to go home! Developing rehabilitation opportunities for older people in Northumberland. Whole systems event report.* Morpeth: Northumberland HAZ

 Case study 1 Northumberland Health Action Zone

Day one began with everyone exploring the patterns of local services that have the potential to deliver or support rehabilitation. Older people brought a different perspective to this exercise, often suggesting rehabilitation opportunities unrecognised by professionals, e.g. tea dances, swimming clubs, exercise groups. The contribution of the professionals was often restricted to naming services run or commissioned by the NHS or social services.

By identifying what was done well and what was done less well by current services, the participants were able to move on to setting possible agendas for change. Thus, in almost every case, people recognised the need to integrate care, through closer partnership working across agency and professional boundaries. Older participants frequently emphasised the lack of rehabilitation opportunities in the community.

Day two began by getting people to imagine how, in an ideal world, they would like to see rehabilitation opportunities improved in three years' time, using the ideas generated in earlier sessions. Various themes emerged, including objectives for systems and individuals, ideas for new services or reshaping existing ones, and changes in individual working practices. Groups of participants then selected a theme and developed an action plan for bringing about the desired changes.

 ## Case study 2 Mid-Hants Primary Care Trust

At a workshop held by mid-Hants Primary Care Trust in November 2001, small groups of participants representing all stakeholders in the care community were given brief case notes. Some examples are shown below:

Case 1

Planned admission for hip replacement. Relatively fit and well. Lives with husband, who is in good health. Retired 10 years ago. From home and back to home.

Case 2

Planned admission for heart bypass operation. Well and in good spirits. Lives alone. Has close friends and relatives. Retired. Played golf until recently. From home and back to home.

Case 3

Planned admission for hip operation. Severe depression, pain. Grown-up son who has mental health problems. Has small home care package. Both have community psychiatric nurse. From home and back to home.

Case 4

Person behaving out of character. Confused. Services contacted by worried neighbours. Lives alone. Managed at home up until now with no problems. From home and back to home.

Case 5

Sufferer from Parkinson's disease, fiercely independent. Lives in sheltered accommodation. Falls over and is found. What happens next?

Case 6

Person is self-funded in dual-registered nursing home. Falls over in the village while out shopping. Has non-insulin dependent, stable diabetes. What happens next?

The cases chosen were based on a mixture of planned and unplanned events, and were prescriptive enough to get the discussion started. Each group was asked to map the likely journey of the client in the existing service system. They then recorded where choice (or a lack of choice) existed, and noted any gaps in services that might affect the care provided. People were encouraged to 'think out of the box', without constraint. Key points from the discussions were fed back to the whole group.

The second session involved each group listing the components of care and support which they would like to see in a redesigned local intermediate care system, including both new services and new ways of working. Each group was given one of the following specific constraints within which to work:

1. New model should be closely aligned with primary care.
2. New model should be closely aligned with secondary care.
3. New model should be closely aligned with the independent sector.
4. No expense spared in developing a new model.
5. New model must be resourced from existing finance.
6. All the staff in the new model will be employed by a single agency.

They reported back to the whole group by drawing a picture of how their new model would work for service users and for staff. The outputs from this workshop informed the development of a new strategy for intermediate care in mid-Hants.

Case study 3 Nuffield Institute for Health

At a workshop run by Nuffield Institute for Health, Leeds University, participants were asked to consider how the rehabilitation needs of older people in a sample area ('Careshire') could be met in ways more closely aligned to the values and principles that ideally underlie care provision. They were given a set of guiding principles, as well as information about current resources in the care community and about the categories of rehabilitation need that the redesigned service model should meet.

As well as shifting the balance of care away from a heavy reliance on institutional settings and towards the community, they were encouraged to make more imaginative use of voluntary and private sector services and to consider changing current ways of working for statutory sector staff.

The task was presented as follows:

> To consider the possible service models needed in this community to provide care for a given range of rehabilitation needs.
>
> ■ Discuss how best to use existing resources.
> ■ Decide what new care models could be developed.
> ■ Discuss what is involved at both strategic and operational levels.
> ■ Identify barriers to change and suggest ways to overcome them.
> ■ Feed key points back to the full group.
>
> Adapted from Nuffield Institute for Health (2001). Accompanying papers, Policy into Practice Seminar Series: 'Intermediate care: rehabilitation, recuperation or warehousing'. West Yorkshire Playhouse, 22 February.

Participants were given information about existing services and resources in the local community (Careshire), details of eight programmes of care that must be provided (Enderby and Stevenson 2000), an outline of the NSF Implementation Framework (Department of Health, 2001b), and the principles that should underpin service. The notes for participants in the workshops are reproduced below:

Careshire – notes for participants

Population	76,000
Area	100 sq mi (260 sq km)
Settlement patterns	One large town
	Some smaller satellite settlements
	Small villages
	Isolated houses/farms
Local resources	Acute hospital
	Community hospital (one 26-bed rehabilitation ward; day hospital)
	Local authority residential rehabilitation unit (nine beds)
	Nursing home rehabilitation unit (four beds)
	Day care centres (two, in voluntary sector)
	17 GP practices (in two primary care groups)
	Occupational therapists (3.5 wte – £92,000)
	Physiotherapists (4.5 wte – £118,000)

Local resources	Rehabilitation assistants (3.2 wte – £45,600)
(continued)	Rehabilitation nurses (2.0 wte – £46,500)
	LA Home Care Service (costs £5.11 per hour)
	'Enhanced' Care Assistants (costs £5.45 per hour)

You are members of Careshire's joint planning group for older people's services.

Using the data above, consider how you will plan and reshape services to meet the needs of the local population for rehabilitation, taking account of national policy and guidance alongside locally agreed values and principles of care.

Assume that there is no new money to invest in intermediate care services.

The needs are defined in terms of eight programmes of care identified in the handout (Enderby and Stevenson, 2000). Thinking broadly and laterally, discuss what, where, how and who. Be sure to take a whole systems approach. Record key issues as these emerge to feed back to the full group at the end of the session.

Adapted from Nuffield Institute for Health (2001), as on p. 55.

What 'whole systems' events can achieve

In the workshops described above, the aim was to help participants widen their perspectives on how rehabilitation and intermediate care can be offered to clients across different care settings and agency and professional boundaries in an integrated way. The discussion should bring out the need for stakeholder involvement in setting and developing the agenda for change, with contributions by older people and by commissioners and providers from health, housing, social care, leisure and recreation in both the statutory and independent sectors.

The debate should not focus solely on intermediate care, but should recognise that it forms part of the continuum of care, and needs to be planned and commissioned in this context.

It is not about:

- commissioning more of the existing services
- renaming existing services without changing their practices
- setting up isolated single services
- adding therapy staff to existing services and calling them 'intermediate care'.

It is about:

- managing change: leading, empowering staff and users, supporting, training
- developing agreements, criteria and protocols on pathways of care
- using Health Act flexibilities – pooled budgets, lead agency, charging policy
- employing an intermediate care co-ordinator
- decision-making and prioritising
- having clear aims for new developments
- developing a single assessment process, involving client-held records that follow people as their condition changes and as they move through the service system
- before introducing change, developing an evaluation framework to test outcomes
- deciding on who could benefit by carrying out local needs assessment, based on categories of care needs, condition/disease specific needs, etc, as illustrated above
- changing the working practices of existing services

- refocusing home care so that it is enabling
- reorganising community staff into teams that include therapists, skilled-up assistants and social services staff
- negotiating for 'missing' therapy skills, such as speech and language therapy, psychology, dietetics and chiropody
- case finding and early intervention, treatment and support, using the voluntary sector to provide, for example, preventative support to combat isolation or enable discharge
- rehabilitation in day care settings
- using housing options.

Figure 9 (below) shows a model of future services, as constructed using a stakeholder day similar to those previously described. It illustrates the pattern of care arrived at – a focus on community rehabilitation teams – and outlines a range of other community-based settings which would form part of the intermediate care system. A single point of access was seen as important, where the assessment and co-ordination of care, as well as the commissioning of services, would be concentrated.

After following such a process, more work is necessary to decide how much of each service component is required to meet the care needs of the local population. However, local stakeholders must agree on a vision and a direction of travel before the detailed service and financial planning, service specification, commissioning and operational planning can proceed.

9 OLDER PEOPLE'S SERVICES IN SHEFFIELD – LAYERS OF SERVICE PROVISION

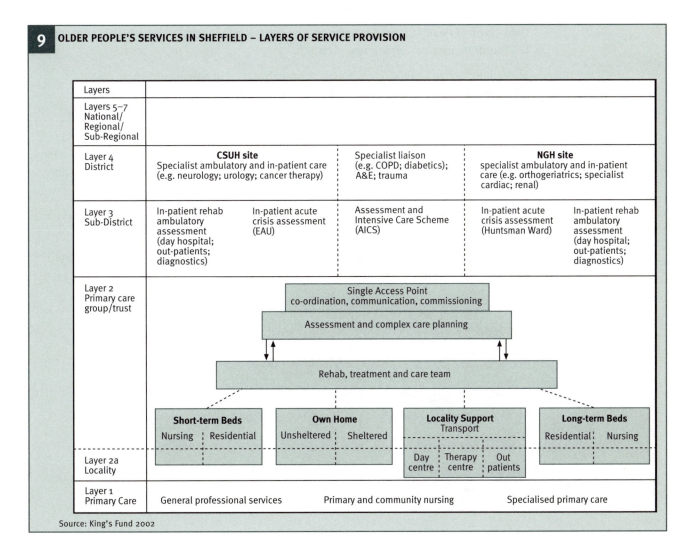

Source: King's Fund 2002

> → **Key points from this section**
> - Begin by agreeing shared values and principles with all stakeholders.
> - Ensure that stakeholders know what is expected in terms of national policy and how this relates to local circumstances.
> - Using one of the available diagnostic tools, analyse how people use existing services, looking for gaps and bottlenecks and checking on whether access is equitable.
> - Once you have established needs, decide upon the services that are required to meet them – rather than trying to fit people into existing services.
> - One of the most effective ways of consulting with stakeholders is to hold a 'whole systems' event.

 ## Further reading

Anderson W, Florin D, Gillam S and Mountford L (2002). *Every voice counts. Primary care organisations and public involvement.* London: King's Fund.

Beech R and Cropper S (2001). *An analytical framework for supporting the planning of intermediate care services.* Report prepared for the R&D Directorate, NHS Executive West Midlands. Available at: www.keele.ac.uk/depts/hm/chpmhmpg.htm

Department of Health (2001). *Continuing care: NHS and local councils' responsibilities.* HSC 2001/015: LAC (2001)18. London: Department of Health.

Department of Health (2001) *Guidance on free nursing care in nursing homes.* HSC 2001/017: LAC (2001)26. London: Department of Health.

McGrath H, George J and Young J (2002). The rehabilitation of older people from ethnic minorities, in Squires A and Hastings M, editors. *Rehabilitation of the older person: a handbook for the multidisciplinary team.* 3rd ed. Cheltenham: Nelson Thornes.

Naish J, Sharples P, Maclaren D, Harvey C, Carter Y, Curtis S, Gilham V, Gregory I, Ball C and Eldridge S (2001). *Partners in information management: multi sectoral information in a primary care group area.* London: Queen Mary and Westfield College, Department of General Practice and Primary Care.

Seargeant J and Steele J (1998). *Consulting the public: guidelines and good practice.* London: Policy Studies Institute.

Stevenson J (1999). *Involving older people in health developments.* Briefing Paper 4. London: King's Fund Programme Developing Rehabilitation Opportunities for Older People.

5 Making practical plans

In order to deliver intermediate care effectively, you may need to redesign the local care system, either wholly or in part. Looking at information about what specific service models can contribute will be helpful. The next step is to set up the appropriate partnership arrangements with other agencies. Then you can start to draw up an action plan that specifies exactly what needs to be done, and who will do it.

This section looks at:
- working with complexity
- which services to offer
- partnership arrangements
- drawing up an action plan.

Working with complexity

When intermediate care services were beginning to be set up, the need for this type of care was so great and existing provision was so limited that, whatever the nature of the service, there were inevitably more potential clients than places. Now that there are many more intermediate care opportunities, however, a more sophisticated approach is needed to planning. In an ideal world, you should be offering a full range of care options in different settings, giving clients a choice of provision. It is therefore important to get a sense of how many people could benefit from each of the potential intermediate care options.

However, there will also be some constraints on what can be done, imposed by local circumstances. It is essential to have a clear picture of all the resources in the local system currently devoted to the care of older people. If pooling of budgets is to be considered, the following must be known:

- which expenditure is fixed and cannot be pooled (e.g. the cost of rehabilitation provision in acute hospitals as part of acute treatment and care programmes)
- which expenditure is flexible and could be pooled (e.g. the cost of care staff employed by health and social care agencies in the community)
- whether there is new money for intermediate care
- whether there are resources that can be moved around the system (e.g. care staff in the community).

Many stakeholders need to be involved in these discussions, as the system can only work if everyone understands how it should work and agrees to tackle any issues that need to be resolved.

Which services to offer

In places where there is a range of stand-alone intermediate care services, it may now be necessary to redesign the whole or parts of the system, in order to use scarce resources more effectively and efficiently.

The balance of care approach

One way of taking your planning forward is to adopt the balance of care approach. This can help you and the other stakeholders to:

■ discuss the potential for changes in service configuration
■ define existing care pathways or create new ones
■ explore the potential for redeploying staff and resources to support different models of care.

The balance of care approach is described as 'a whole systems methodology which incorporates both the conceptual and practical elements of setting out local strategies and mapping out service development plans' (Forte *et al.*, 2002). Several local projects undertaken by members of the Balance of Care Group have focused on planning intermediate care.

A simplified version of the balance of care model is shown in Figure 10 (below), which describes combinations of services to meet specific types of need. For example, people in the 'supported discharge' category might include arthritic patients recovering from a fall, while those classified as 'rehab/recovery' would include people recovering from a stroke.

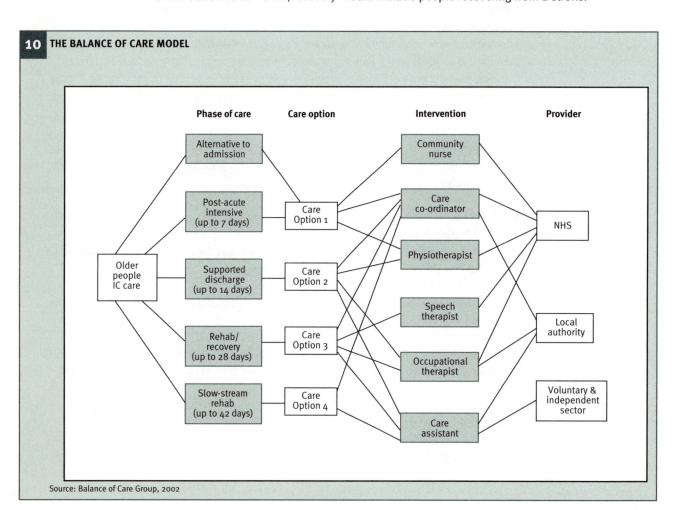

10 THE BALANCE OF CARE MODEL

Source: Balance of Care Group, 2002

The medical and social characteristics of clients can be defined in terms of the assessment criteria used to determine care pathways, though at a much higher level of aggregation, since the approach is concerned only with resource requirements, rather than the details of the care to be provided. Note that there may be more than one care option for any given group of patients.

These pathways will in turn require different combinations of skills-based services, as well as 'bricks and mortar' facilities – some of which may be provided by more than one agency in a locality.

An example of the kind of information that the balance of care approach can generate is given in Table 2 (below). These particular data capture the care inputs identified by local stakeholders as being necessary for delivering a new model of care to a group of people broadly categorised as needing post-acute care for four weeks. The number of clients is derived from an analysis of local data, and the costings used are the local costs for each element of care. Similar data are generated for redesigned care pathways and packages for each broad group of intermediate care clients.

TABLE 2: MODEL OF CARE FOR PEOPLE NEEDING POST-ACUTE CARE FOR FOUR WEEKS

	C3 – Post acute (less than 28 days)			Patients:	52
Unit Cost:	£1,968	£2,727	£2,700	£	**Totals**
Allocation:	27%	29%	44%		100%
Allocated Patients:	14	15	23	0	52
Code Service Description	**Fit Carer**	**Frail Carer**	**No Carer**		**Cost**
S1 EMI day hospital (days)					£
S2 Community nurse (hours)	2	2	2		£1,473
S3 Community nurse (night service) (hours)		2	14		£6,400
S4 Community psych. nurse (hours)					£
S5 Specialist services (nrs; diet; etc.) (hours)	1	1	1		£808
S6 Rehab beds (days)	14	18	14		£61,938
S7 Voluntary sector support (hours)	6	12	6		£6,842
S8 OT (hours)	3	3	3		£1,936
S9 Physiotherapy (hours)	3	3	3		£2,005
S10 Rehab asst (hours)	12	12	12		£9,672
S11 Day hospital (days)	1	1	1		£7,332
S12 GP (hours)	1	1	1		£2,600
S13 Nursing home (days)					£
S14 Night sitting service (hours)	3.5	7	14		£8,075
S15 Dietetics (hours)	1	1	1		£52
S16 Home care (personal) (hours)	7	15	21		£8,050
S17 Care manager (social worker) (hours)	2	4	3		£2,874
S18 Domestic services (hours)	4	10	14		£4,482
S19 Day centre (days)	2	2	2		£3,536
S20 Meals (meals)		20	14		£2,457

Source: Balance of Care Group

The balance of care method is supported by computer software enabling the data to be aggregated to predict the required human and financial resources. By comparing the data on current resources with the predicted requirements, you can see where potential shortfalls or surpluses might occur with the new patterns of service. It is also possible to try out changes to particular aspects of the pathways or care components, so allowing you to see the effect of these changes on the overall requirements.

This approach has shown that, if new models of care to support more people in the community are to be delivered, some current staff will need to move to different roles and settings. It has also demonstrated the potential contribution to new models of care that generic rehabilitation assistants can make, thus reducing the demand for scarce specialist therapy staff.

Information about individual service models

@ Available at:
www.doh.gov.uk/swro/
intermediatecare.pdf;
SWRO home page:
www.doh.gov.uk/swro/
olderpeopleservices.htm).

There is much more information available about individual service models, either from the literature or direct from service providers. The former NHS Executive South West/Social Services Inspectorate South West Regional Office (SWRO) maintained a record of 'the various schemes and projects ... now available which enable the NHS, Housing, Social Services and the Independent Sector, separately or together, to contribute towards supporting more people closer to home' (NHS Executive South West/Social Services Inspectorate South West Regional Office, 2002). @

Schemes are grouped into the following categories:

- promoting independence
- arrangements to improve practice in assessment
- preventing avoidable admissions
- improving the use of hospital and long-term care resources
- developments in rehabilitation
- other services.

For each entry, there is a brief description of the service and its objectives, plus details of staffing, referral arrangements and availability, and funding details.

@ See: www.doh.gov.uk/swro/
characteristics.pdf

Also on the website is the document *Intermediate care: classification of terms* (*see* Appendix 3, p. 106). This complements the intermediate care circular; it gives entries for specific services, describing purpose and aims, typical patients and conditions, effectiveness and evidence, and good practice. @

@ See: www.doh.gov.uk/swro/
olderpeopleservices

The website also contains the document 'Models of care that aim to prevent inappropriate hospital admissions'. This resource lists four models (Appendix 4, p. 110), describing the service on offer, the range of potential service providers and the staffing requirements: @

- community team, health-led
- community team, social care-led
- hospital-based team
- residential-based team.

The paper emphasises the need to see alternatives to admission as part of a continuum of care, with clear criteria for referral and adequate arrangements for discharge back into community-based services where required.

Partnership arrangements

The Section 31 partnership arrangements in the Health Act 1999 give NHS and local authorities the flexibility to be able to respond effectively to improve services, either by joining up existing services, or developing new, co-ordinated services, and to work with other organisations to fulfil this ... The partnership arrangements are pooled funds and the delegation of functions – lead commissioning and integrated provision.

@ Available at:
www.doh.gov.uk/jointunit/
pship1.htm#pooled

Department of Health (2000c). *Guidance on the Health Act Section 31 partnership arrangements*. London: Department of Health. @

As we have seen, the Department of Health expects that 'pooled budgets and the use of other Health Act flexibilities will be the norm in arranging intermediate care services' (Department of

www.doh.gov.uk/jointunit/
notifications.pdf

Health, 2000a). So far, however, few agencies seem to have formally pooled their budgets for developing intermediate care, to judge from the list of notifications on the Department of Health website.

Monitoring of health and social care partnerships since the Health Act 1999 has shown that many agencies are unwilling to pool large budgets for caring for older people (Banks, 2002). They fear that it will limit their room to manoeuvre financially or that they may pick up their partners' financial deficit. However, there are examples of smaller sums being put into pooled budgets. These may indicate a willingness to explore the potential of flexible arrangements, perhaps using the new funds that the Government has earmarked for the further development of intermediate care.

Available only at:
www.doh.gov.uk/jointunit/
guidance.htm

It is also possible that people do not yet understand how to go about pooling their budgets. Detailed guidance from the Health and Social Care Joint Unit, Department of Health describes who can contribute to a pooled budget, what can be contributed and how large the pooled fund should be, and emphasises the need to agree on aims, outcomes and targets.

The information is arranged as follows:

- **purpose of partnership arrangements**
- **the pooled funding arrangement**
  managing the pooled budget
  audit
- **delegation of function**
  lead commissioning
  integrated provision
- **notification process**
- **consultation**
- **governance arrangements**
- **performance management**
- **clinical governance**
- **best value**
- **inspection arrangements**
- **assessment arrangements and eligibility criteria**
- **direct payments**
- **complaints**
- **financial arrangements**
  charging
  VAT
  local authority/health body joint stores and VAT
- **boundaries**
- **exit strategies, disputes and termination of partnership arrangements**
- **workforce issues.**

The Department of Health provides practical guidance on using the Health Act flexibilities, in the form of a checklist for local authority and health staff. This is not intended as a definitive framework for using the flexibilities, but rather as 'a prompt, to set out some baseline questions applicable to partnerships but subject to local circumstances and intended outcomes'. The checklist is shown in Appendix 5, p. 112.

www.doh.gov.uk/jointunit/
phhaf.htm

Joint funding of new intermediate care services is much more common. In these cases, partner agencies must make formal arrangements to ensure proper accountability and use of joint funds.

Drawing up an action plan

Once a change has been agreed, you should develop an action plan describing the tasks that need to be done to achieve the agreed objective.

One method successfully used in workshops with intermediate care stakeholders enables participants to organise the tasks into a logical sequence (*see* 'What "whole systems" events can achieve', p. 56). The tasks are recorded on a chart designed for the purpose. First, it is important to be very clear about the objective to be achieved. This is the 'bullseye' – the target to aim for – and is recorded in the associated text box.

Participants are then asked to break down into four (or more) stages what has to be done to reach the target. Starting with Stage 1, the various tasks required to achieve that stage are listed in order. Before moving on to list the tasks in Stage 2, participants must agree on how it will be recognised that the first stage has been successfully completed. This 'evidence' statement is recorded in the circle at the foot of the Stage 1 column.

Once the tasks in the final column have been listed, the target should have been achieved.

As the exercise is about the tasks to be done, it is important that people should not be side-tracked into trying to solve any problems encountered along the way. Inevitably, some of these problems will be mentioned: you should acknowledge them but not dwell on them – they should be 'parked' so as not to disrupt the action planning.

When undertaking action planning using this format, it is a good idea to record stages and tasks using adhesive notes that can be moved around the chart, as there will inevitably be changes in the order of actions as the exercise progresses.

Figure 11 (opposite) is an example of an action plan to agree a vision and an implementation plan for reshaping a service system to meet intermediate care needs.

Key milestones are often the points at which the vision and subsequent development plans are signed up to by the stakeholder agencies. This often involves submitting papers to management boards or committees. If the timetable for these key decision points is known in advance, it will help you indicate the time needed to obtain high-level agreement to planned change.

By adding time scales and allocating responsibilities for managing the process and for progressing each task, it is possible to generate a work plan for meeting the agreed objective – although, of course, implementation rarely proceeds as smoothly in the real world as it does on paper. Although some goals and tasks will inevitably change along the way, this kind of action planning can help stakeholders to agree a way forward.

11 **SAMPLE ACTION PLAN**

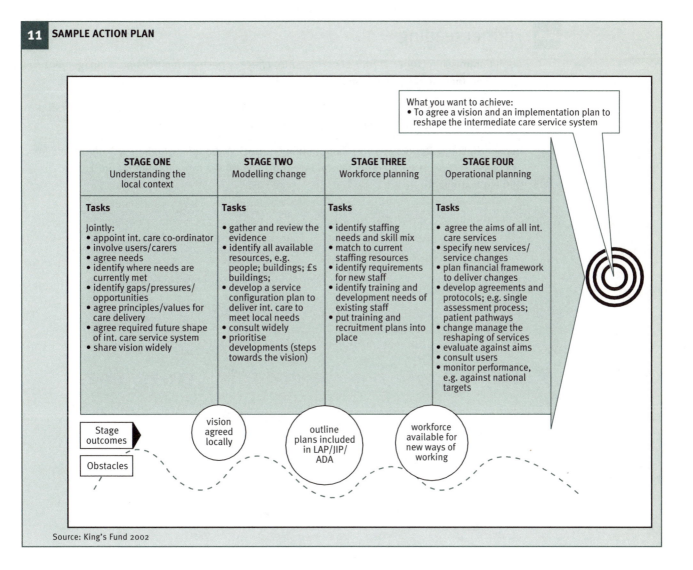

Source: King's Fund 2002

→ Key points from this section

■ **Begin by redesigning the local care system so that it can deliver intermediate care effectively. Try using the balance of care approach which compares care inputs with client needs.**

■ **Inform your service development by consulting information about what specific service models can contribute.**

■ **Set up partnership arrangements with appropriate agencies.**

■ **Draw up an action plan that specifies exactly what needs to be done and who will do it.**

Further reading

Audit Commission (1998). *A fruitful partnership: effective partnership working.* Management paper. London: Audit Commission.

Hardy B, Hudson B and Waddington E (2000). *What makes a good partnership? A partnership assessment tool.* Leeds: Nuffield Institute for Health.

Hudson B, Young R, Hardy B, and Glendinning C (2001). *National evaluation of notifications for use of the Section 31 partnership flexibilities of the Health Act 1999.* Interim report. Leeds: Nuffield Institute for Health.

6 Putting intermediate care plans into practice

Putting your plans into practice will require strong leadership and effective management of change: you will need to engage the support of existing staff and explore new ways of working. Medical input to the new services will have to be arranged. The resulting system should be flexible enough to meet the needs of all users and to ensure continuity of care. This may involve contracting out some functions to the independent sector. You will also have to agree on a single assessment process with all stakeholders. Finally, it will be necessary to decide who will co-ordinate the intermediate care.

This section looks at:
- the success factors
- change management
- the operational implications of change
- redesigning existing intermediate care systems
- contracting for intermediate care with the independent sector
- assessment
- the role of the intermediate care co-ordinator.

The success factors

The Department of Health (Department of Health, 2002a) has compiled a list of the factors it regards as essential for success in developing intermediate care (Appendix 6, p. 116), which can be summarised as follows.

Vision, drive and leadership are top of the list. They include the ability to see beyond existing service patterns and the drive to surmount the many obstacles to change that will be encountered. Strong leadership is needed at various levels in the care system, to spread the vision and to encourage others to subscribe to the agenda for change.

Commitment at senior level is essential 'to ensure that the appropriate level of resources is committed, that difficult organisational decisions are taken and that those delivering services at the sharp end are empowered to work flexibly in the interests of service users'. Significantly, the list recognises that 'new ways of working need both permission and protection'.

Research into older people and whole systems working currently in progress (Audit Commission, in press) suggests that:

A series of whole system competencies, or behaviours, are beginning to emerge, including:

- modelling and acting as a champion for partnership behaviour, so that working across boundaries is seen as an organisational norm
- developing healthy relationships with peers across the system to build a leadership team
- taking joint responsibility, with other members of the leadership team, for delivering improved services and holding each other to account for inaction or failure
- supporting actions which benefit older people and the system as a whole, even if these are not the most favourable for their own organisation

- creating an organisational culture in which whole system working can flourish
- identifying 'win/win' solutions to shared difficulties, where possible
- managing the political context (for example, by addressing the concerns of elected members)
- agreeing and communicating consistent messages about the system's values, vision and priorities, in particular by placing older people at the centre
- valuing staff who work in a whole system way
- sharing financial risk.

Audit Commission (in press). *Older people and whole systems working* (working title). London: Audit Commission.

The idea of the members of a leadership team holding each other to account is significant in the context of whole systems engagement, as is the recognition that 'middle managers and team leaders also have a key role in mirroring the leadership behaviours listed above, to ensure that consistent values, messages and approaches are cascaded throughout the system'. The study also highlights the important leadership role of elected members in championing services for older people (Audit Commission, in press).

Change management

Action planning is not intended to take account of problems. However, reshaping services across an entire care system must by definition encounter many obstacles, and therefore you must be prepared to manage complex change.

There is a vast literature on the subject of change management, but here we will limit ourselves to giving extracts from two publications by the National Co-ordinating Centre for NHS Service Delivery and Organisation. The first is a literature review to familiarise NHS staff with the thinking about change management originating from other disciplines (Iles and Sutherland, 2001). The second is a summary of the key lessons that aims to help managers and professionals bridge the gap between commitment to change and action (National Co-ordinating Centre for NHS Service Delivery and Organisation, 2001).

These publications were commissioned for staff working towards the ambitious agenda for change set out in the NHS Plan (Department of Health, 2000a). But the advice they give is equally relevant to people reshaping rehabilitation and intermediate care anywhere in the health and social care system.

Managing change – the reality

This first extract is from the summary of key lessons (National Co-ordinating Centre for NHS Service Delivery and Organisation, 2001):

Change is often imposed upon managers to meet priorities that differ from the priorities perceived as most important by the key opinion formers within the unit or organisation – in particular, the clinicians.

There is a tension between instruction to 'gain ownership' of a particular change initiative and the instruction to deliver the change quickly.

Priorities change, and so a change programme may be overtaken by other initiatives.

Amid new initiatives, it is very easy to lose sight of the original objectives of a change programme – and only too easy to implement a series of actions that may no longer be the most relevant.

Many staff members are cynical about consultation processes, born of experience of 'pseudo consultation' and of change associated with cutting costs.

Change of any kind inevitably involves some kind of loss, which may need to be addressed.

There is scepticism about change techniques imported from the private sector. Clinicians will value evidence about the virtues of a change in a form with which they are familiar, but this may not be available or appropriate.

There is an opportunity cost, measured in lost patient care, associated with time spent planning and implementing change.

Managers tend to stay in post for shorter periods than their clinical colleagues and thus are not able to see a change programme through from start to finish, nor to learn from the results.

Adapted from the key lessons summarised in National Co-ordinating Centre for NHS Service Delivery and Organisation (2001). *Making informed decisions on change.* London: NCC SDO R&D.

Why do we need to change?

The following pages comprise a series of adapted extracts from the original literature review from Iles and Sutherland (2001):

Getting to grips with the question

Many models can help people to explore either directly or indirectly the rationale for change. We look at only one such model here – SWOT analysis.

SWOT (strengths, weaknesses, opportunities, threats) focuses attention on the match – or lack of match – between what the organisation is geared up to offer and what the world outside it needs and wants. In doing so, it encourages people to see their own organisation, group or team from a range of different perspectives. Some of these perspectives are likely to be unfamiliar.

In the NHS, as in other complex systems, it is only too easy to look inwards much more frequently than outwards – or for attention to be focused on certain types of drivers, such as policy directives or performance indicators. But the real answers to the question 'why do we need to change?' lie in identifying and reflecting on the gaps between what is currently being offered and what is likely to be needed in the next few years.

Adapted from Iles V and Sutherland K (2001). *Organisational change.* London: NCC SDO R&D.

SWOT analysis

Description
SWOT is an acronym for examining an operation's strengths, weaknesses, opportunities and threats, and using the result to identify priorities for action (Ansoff, 1965). The main principle underlying SWOT is that internal and external factors must be considered simultaneously, when identifying aspects of an organisation that need to be changed. Strengths and weaknesses are internal to the organisation; opportunities and threats are external.

Use
Many managers and health professionals will have experience of working with this framework. A team or other sub-unit of an organisation writes down its mission or purpose. Keeping this mission in mind, they then identify all their strengths and weaknesses ... They do the same for opportunities and threats ... On its own this information is rarely helpful or usable, and must

be considered further. This requires the asking of further questions about each of the factors listed under the four headings.

For strengths and weaknesses, the questions asked are:

1. What are the consequences of this? Do they help or hinder us in achieving our mission?

If the factor does genuinely help the achievement of the mission (and only if the positive impact on the mission is convincing) then indeed it is a strength. Similarly if, but only if, it hinders achievement of the mission it is a weakness.

2. What are the causes of this strength (or weakness)?

For opportunities and threats, the questions are slightly different:

1. What impact is this likely to have on us? Will it help or hinder us in achieving our mission?

Again, only if the opportunity helps the team achieve the mission can it be considered such; even if it causes the world to be a nicer place, but fails to impact on the team's ability to achieve its mission, it will not be an opportunity for these purposes.

2. What must we do to respond to this opportunity or threat?

The analyst now reflects on the mission and all four components, paying particular attention to the causes of the strengths and weaknesses, and to the responses required to the opportunities and threats, and links together common threads into a set of priorities for the team to address.

Commentary
SWOT needs to be used carefully and with the end in mind rather than as a process in its own right.

Adapted from Iles and Sutherland (2001), as above.

Who and what can change?

Below is Iles and Sutherland's description of three specific approaches to change management:

- the technique of force field analysis
- a method of analysing people's readiness to change
- ways of securing individual behaviour change.

Getting to grips with the question

Since its earliest days, the NHS has been characterised by almost constant structural change. Change of this kind has resolved some problems at some times, but has left many other deep-seated problems untouched.

There is increasing recognition that people – individuals, teams and workforces – offer the key to lasting change in the health service. People deliver health services to people. They do this within a system that either helps or hinders them. Managers and other leaders are looking for ways in which they can manage resources and integrate a range of processes, plans and initiatives while acting on the principle that 'people should be seen as a way of solving problems ... rather than part of the problem and either taken for granted or more rigidly controlled' (NHS Executive, 2000).

Many will be concerned, therefore, to know more about working with others to create an adaptable workforce of the kind described in the NHS Plan (Department of Health, 2000a) well led and fit for practice and purpose. There is likely to be particular interest in the following issues:

■ What helps or hinders people working together to achieve change?
■ How can lessons from the change effort be shared as constructively and widely as possible?
■ What kinds of change intervention are particularly 'people-friendly'?

Adapted from Iles and Sutherland (2001), as above.

Force field analysis

Iles and Sutherland continue on the subject of force field analysis:

Description

Force field analysis (Lewin, 1951) is a diagnostic technique which has been applied to ways of looking at the variables involved in determining whether organisational change will occur. It is based on the concept of 'forces', a term which refers to the perceptions of people in the organisation about a particular factor and its influences.

Driving forces are those forces affecting a situation and which are attempting to push it in a particular direction. These forces tend to initiate change or keep it going. Restraining forces are forces acting to restrain or decrease the driving forces. A state of equilibrium is reached when the sum of the driving forces equals the sum of the restraining forces (*see* Figure 12, below).

Lewin formulated three fundamental assertions about force fields and change:

1. Increasing the driving forces results in an increase in the resisting forces; the current equilibrium does not change but is maintained under increased tension.
2. Reducing resisting forces is preferable because it allows movement towards the desired state, without increasing tension.
3. Group norms are an important force in resisting and shaping organisational change.

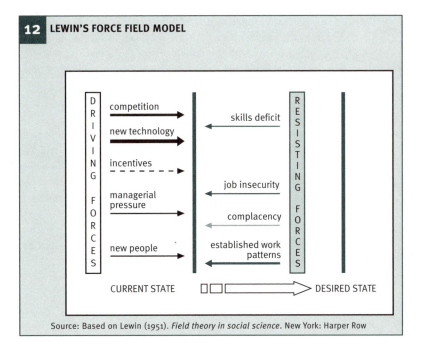

12 **LEWIN'S FORCE FIELD MODEL**

Source: Based on Lewin (1951). *Field theory in social science*. New York: Harper Row

Use

Once change priorities have been agreed, using methods from the last two clusters, a force field analysis can be used to identify actions that would enhance their successful implementation.

Adapted from Iles and Sutherland (2001), as above.

The authors continue:

Commentary

For the model to be of use, the forces need to be identified perceptively, rigorously and objectively, and the means identified of addressing the resisting forces need to be creative.

Many practising managers will be able to reflect on occasions in their own experience when they have aimed to increase the driving forces, rather than reduce the resisting ones, and have increased the resistance and the tension as a result.

Readiness and capability

Individual resistance to change is widely recognised as a huge barrier to successful implementation of new ways of working. Some strategies for overcoming such resistance are described in the following review:

Description

Early on in the change process, managers need to identify which specific groups and individuals will be required to support the change if the change is to be successful. When they have done so, they can determine the readiness and capability of these individuals and groups to enact the roles required of them in the change process. Understanding the readiness involves analysing attitudes: willingness, motives and aims.

Adapted from Iles and Sutherland (2001), as above.

They continue:

Commitment, enrolment and compliance

Where a change must be implemented from the outside ... that is, when it has not been defined as necessary by the people involved, then it is unlikely to succeed (that is, yield the full results of which people have ambitions) unless some of those involved are in favour of it. Several observers have suggested that not everyone needs to support a change, and that not everybody needs to support it in the same extent.

Description and use

In *The fifth discipline* (1990), Senge talks of the difference between commitment, enrolment and compliance, suggesting that while it is more pleasant (and reassuring) to have considerable commitment, it is not necessary for everyone to be fully signed up as this. There exist a number of positions along a continuum, along which players may position themselves in response to proposed action and change, as illustrated in the box opposite.

Senge suggests analysing what level of support is required from each of the players and directing energy to achieve that, rather than at trying to persuade everybody to 'commit'.

COMMITMENT, ENROLMENT AND COMPLIANCE

Disposition	Players' response to the change
Commitment	■ want change to happen and will work to make it happen ■ willing to create whatever structure, systems and frameworks are necessary to make it work
Enrolment	■ want change to happen and will devote time and energy to making it happen within given frameworks ■ act within the spirit of the frameworks
Genuine compliance	■ see the virtue in what is proposed, do what is asked of them and think proactively about what is needed ■ act within the letter of the framework
Formal compliance	■ can describe the benefits of what is proposed and are not hostile to them ■ do what they are asked but no more. Stick to the letter of the framework
Grudging compliance	■ do not accept that there are benefits to what is proposed and do not go along with it ■ do enough of what is asked of them not to jeopardise position ■ voice opposition and hope for failure ■ interpret the letter of the framework
Non-compliance	■ do not accept that there are benefits and that there is nothing to lose by opposing the proposition ■ will not do what is asked of them ■ work outside framework
Apathy	■ neither in support not in opposition to the proposal, just serving time ■ don't care about framework

Adapted from Senge P (1990). *The fifth discipline: the art and practice of the learning organisation*. London: Doubleday/Century Press

Iles and Sutherland continue:

In health care organisations, a range of specific interventions has been used to try to change individual clinicians' behaviour. These include:

- educational outreach
- audit and feedback
- access to local opinion leaders
- patient-specific reminders
- continuing medical education
- dissemination of guidelines.

Their effectiveness in securing change in clinical behaviour may provide some insights for those managing change in a wider context throughout the organisation.
Iles and Sutherland (2001), as above.

Securing individual behaviour change

Effective health care (NHS Centre for Reviews and Dissemination, 1999) provides a comprehensive review of published accounts of methods and approaches that have sought to secure change in the behaviour of health care professionals.

Its main conclusions are as follows:

- Most interventions are effective under some circumstances; none is effective under all circumstances.
- A diagnostic analysis of the individual and the context must be performed before selecting a method for altering individual practitioner behaviour.
- Interventions based on assessment of potential barriers are more likely to be effective.
- Multifaceted interventions targeting different barriers to change are more likely to be effective than single interventions.
- Educational outreach is generally effective in changing prescribing behaviour in North American settings. Ongoing trials will provide rigorous evidence about the effectiveness of this approach in UK settings.
- Reminder systems are generally effective for a range of behaviours.
- Audit and feedback, opinion leaders and other interventions have mixed effects and should be used selectively.
- Passive dissemination when used alone is unlikely to result in behaviour change. However, this approach may be useful for raising awareness of research messages.

Iles and Sutherland (2001), as above.

The operational implications of change

Fundamental to the reforms set out in the NHS Plan is the improvement of partnership working. We need to find new ways of working between health and social care that will 'remove the outdated institutional barriers' (Department of Health, 2000a) and provide a seamless service to older people. Services should no longer stand alone. Intermediate care must be integrated into a whole system of care including primary and secondary health care, health and social care in the community, and the statutory and independent sectors.

Operationally, this has two major implications. First, new patterns of care will involve complex multi-sectoral work, with all that this implies for changing ways of working. Second, new understandings and agreements are needed about the ways in which people will move through the care system and who will be involved in their care at which points.

New ways of working

Team-based working is one obvious response to this new agenda. We have seen a plethora of new teams set up to support the delivery of intermediate care. However, in some instances insufficient time and effort have been devoted to team building and staff development. It is not enough simply to tell staff that they now work as part of a team – time must be set aside to let the new team develop a shared understanding of its goals and change its working practices.

Health care teams

The Centre for Health Service Organisation Research at Aston University has published a report on the effectiveness of 400 health care teams (Borrill *et al.*, 2001). Three further documents provide managers and team members with information to help teams to meet the new challenges they face (Borrill *et al.*, 2001c; Borrill and West, 2001a; Borrill and West, 2001b;).

See the evidence on the value of team working cited in 'What research exists on the operational aspects of intermediate care?', p. 34.

The document *How good is your team? A guide for team members* (Borrill and West, 2001b), discusses team working and the general conditions required to promote it effectively. It includes an audit tool that enables teams to assess how well they are working together and gives advice on how they can improve their team working.

Another document by Borrill and West (2001a), *Developing team working in health care. A guide for managers*, can also be used to help teams meet the new challenges. It describes the importance of team working in organisations and the general conditions required to promote it. An audit tool is provided for assessing how well an organisation is doing in providing an environment conducive to team working. There is guidance on how to improve team working by developing the systems and procedures required to support it. A second audit tool can be used to assess how team leaders carry out their role and gives advice on how to lead teams effectively.

Borrill and West *et al.* (2001c) found that teams that include many different professional groups deliver better-quality patient care and introduce more innovations When teams work well together, alternative and competing perspectives are carefully discussed, leading to better quality decisions about patient care.

The study also cited, as a benefit of good team working, the fact that 'people are much clearer about what their jobs entail because team working enables good communication and detailed negotiation of effective work roles' (Borrill *et al.*, 2001c). It is easier to build a shared understanding of the work, and then to develop appropriate processes for delivering high quality care.

Rehabilitation/intermediate care teams

In the past, rehabilitation teams were often set up quickly with limited short-term funding. As a consequence, they frequently had a limited number of staff. Typically, a 'winter pressures' team might have an occupational therapist, a physiotherapist and some administrative support.

However, if we look at the development of, for example, community rehabilitation teams, a pattern emerges of teams that grow in size and expand their areas of expertise as their potential to offer a different model of care is recognised locally and more funding becomes available.

There are examples of teams that have either recruited dedicated staff or made local arrangements for speedy access to a number of other specialists/generalists, such as:

- district nurses
- community psychiatric nurses – many older people using rehabilitation or intermediate care exhibit symptoms of dementia or confusion
- psychologists – motivation is critical to the success of rehabilitation, but many individuals exhibit signs of depression that need to be treated
- speech and language therapists
- rehabilitation/care assistants (*see* 'The evolving role of the rehabilitation assistant, overleaf)
- specialist/generalist medical cover (*see* 'Access to medical cover' overleaf)
- chiropodists

- dieticians
- pharmacists
- care and repair staff
- home economists.

Many intermediate care initiatives have struggled to recruit and retain staff. There are recognised shortages of suitably qualified and experienced staff in many, if not all, of the professions essential to delivering intermediate care. Making the best use of skills and time is therefore paramount. In this respect, it is important to:

- avoid duplication of effort
- work flexibly
- increase the skills of care staff who lack professional qualifications so that they can undertake day-to-day support of clients using a rehabilitation approach.

The evolving role of the rehabilitation assistant

A variety of approaches have been taken to developing the role of the rehabilitation assistant:

Increased use of specialist assistants
Some teams have increased their use of assistants who practise a particular type of therapy, such as occupational therapy and physiotherapy. This approach has a long history, such as in day hospitals or clinics within the NHS.

Blurring of roles
In some teams, roles have been blurred so that the assistant in question becomes a 'therapy assistant', working to individual care plans agreed by the multidisciplinary team with the client.

Increased use of generic care assistants
Other teams have chosen to offer day-to-day support to implement individual care plans through generic care assistants. In most instances, these assistants act more like special home care workers. Although they are trained to provide support, the emphasis is on enabling rather than doing things for the client. They are employed either as team members or as social services home care staff, often linked to specific rehabilitation teams.

Shifting towards enabling/supporting
Some social services departments have recognised the need to shift the ethos of the home care service towards such an enabling and supportive role. To this end, they are running training programmes for the entire home care workforce.

Access to medical cover

A variety of approaches have been evolved to ensure that intermediate care clients have timely and appropriate access to medical cover. These range from including a doctor in the team to commissioning dedicated consultant sessions (Portsmouth CRT, personal communication).

Intermediate care and specialist medical assessment

The following extract from *Intermediate care: moving forward* (Department of Health, 2002a) outlines the different models for access to medical cover:

> The aim of intermediate care services is to offer a genuine choice of care setting for older people. However, there is an associated responsibility to ensure that, whatever the setting, the medical component of care is consistent and of high quality. The medical contribution to

intermediate care services will depend on local circumstances but is likely to include input from one or more of the following:

- consultant geriatrician and psychogeriatrician
- consultant community geriatrician
- general practitioner, some with a specialist interest in older people
- staff grade specialist in older people.

Ideally, the specialist doctor should be integral to the intermediate care team. But, as a minimum expectation, there should be locally agreed procedures for specialist medical assessments such as ready access to local day hospitals and elderly care/psychiatric out-patient clinics.

The specialist medical contribution requires particular attention for an intermediate care service incorporating an admission avoidance component. Here, failure to identify underlying acute illnesses, and other important conditions, is an obvious concern. Admission avoidance intermediate care services based in casualty or on medical assessment units (MAUs) have an advantage in that serious (e.g. fractures) and life threatening (e.g. acute myocardial infarction) conditions will have been excluded. However, these units are rarely an appropriate setting for a full medical assessment of older people, and procedures for secondary referrals for specialist medical assessment (such as the day hospital or out-patient clinic) should be clearly established.

Community-based admission avoidance services (such as direct admission to a nursing home or home-based care) should similarly not disadvantage an older person as far as a specialist medical assessment is concerned. Indeed, these patients could be particularly vulnerable as they bypass the usual medical health care services. Once again, agreed local arrangements for routine, rapid access to a specialist medical assessment should be established.

Adapted from Department of Health (2002a). *Intermediate care: moving forward*. London: Department of Health.

Redesigning existing intermediate care systems

Where there have been isolated developments of rehabilitation and intermediate care, it may now be desirable to pool all the resources used by these services and to consider whether there are more efficient ways of organising care in an integrated way to meet a range of needs. For example, community teams set up to facilitate early hospital discharge often run in parallel with teams that avoid hospital admission. Many of their roles and skills are common and, depending on local circumstances, it may now be more effective to combine them.

Patient/user pathways

Understanding the current patient/user pathways can help to highlight gaps or pressure points in a care system. Care pathway development is important in creating new ways of providing care and in promoting agreement on the most appropriate ways to meet the needs of particular client groups. There is, however, scope for confusion between two different concepts of 'pathway': patient pathways and integrated care pathways.

An integrated care pathway is an outline plan of anticipated clinical practice for a client group who share a particular diagnosis or set of symptoms. It provides a multidisciplinary template of the plan of care (based on guidelines and evidence), leading each patient towards a desired objective (Middleton and Roberts, 2000). Thus, integrated care pathways have been developed to promote consistency in the provision of evidence-based patterns of care for particular groups of people, often in a single-service setting, e.g. acute hospital care of people who have suffered a stroke.

Here, we refer to the patient pathway – the route that an individual takes physically through a care system. This will sometimes involve transfers between settings and sometimes transfers between agencies and/or professionals. Typically, an older person might be admitted to an acute hospital bed from home as an emergency case after becoming ill or falling. Once acute treatment is completed and the person's condition is stable, they might move on to a residential intermediate care unit before returning home, or they could go home with the support of a community rehabilitation team.

A patient pathway must have clear criteria governing the admission and discharge of a person to and from any service. These criteria must reflect the aims of the service in question. Service inputs, especially the staffing levels and the skills mixture, must be appropriate for providing care that meets the needs of the client group.

The assessment process that determines which clients are suitable for which part of the intermediate care service system must be robust enough to select people for particular services or settings where their individual needs can best be met (*see* 'Assessment', p. 81). Their needs will change, so there must be regular reviews. The aim is to provide the right care to the right person at the right time according to their needs and taking account of their preferences.

The literature reports a tendency for rehabilitation pathways to be determined more by the services available in the area than by the abilities and needs of the individuals concerned, as in, for example, Herbert *et al.* (2000). When redesigning the intermediate care system, you must ensure that a range of settings is available to meet different needs, and that clients are not obliged to follow preordained routes through the system, if their needs can be met more acceptably elsewhere. In other words, the system must be flexible.

Consulting clients and carers

You should ensure that clients and carers are involved in decisions about their needs and how these will be met. Researchers have found considerable variations in the amount of information provided. For example, Herbert *et al.* (2000) found that much of the information-giving process was perceived as passive, with fitter patients feeling better informed than frailer older people.

Continuity of care

The transfer of people between services or settings as their needs change must be carefully managed, to ensure that continuity of care is maintained. Individual records and personal care plans must go with the person. This must link in with the local Single Assessment Process (Department of Health, 2001a). Information technology (IT) solutions to the problems of rapid and timely data transfer are being explored in many areas (*see* 'Assessment', p. 81).

Careful system design is required in certain key areas, such as arrangements for timely transport, the supply of medicines and equipment, and organising any necessary adaptations to the person's home before their return. There must be protocols and agreements to cover these arrangements.

The responsibility for managing the system to ensure that the provision of care and any transfers between services are timely and appropriate lies with the intermediate care co-ordinator (Wilson and Stevenson, 2001). *See* 'The role of the intermediate care co-ordinator', p. 84.

Contracting for intermediate care with the independent sector

To help commissioners draw up comprehensive service agreements, the Department of Health has published a guide to contracting for intermediate care services as a basis for local contracts with independent providers. Separate guides provide model contracts for intermediate care in three settings:

Available only at:
www.doh.gov.uk/
intermediatecare/
index.htm#guide

- residential intermediate care
- intermediate day rehabilitation services
- domiciliary intermediate care.

Each guide:

- emphasises the importance of clear agreement on roles and expectations between commissioners and providers
- identifies the areas to be addressed to ensure that patients/users receive a safe and appropriate service, with particular emphasis on areas of risk
- provides a sound contractual agreement that delivers value for money.

For ease of use, each of the contracts is reproduced in its entirety in the guide, avoiding the need for extensive cross-referencing. Each of the three types of contract is presented in a two-column format. The left-hand column lists the issues that commissioners and providers need to take account of in their contracts. The right-hand column contains suggested paragraphs that might be used to address the issues within a local contract.

Commissioners can draw on this menu of suggested paragraphs to suit local needs. The entire set of paragraphs constitutes a model contract that local commissioners may wish to use as it stands. Alternatively, a 'bespoke' contract can be built up by excluding, modifying or adding paragraphs.

Irrespective of the type of contract, you should aim to address all the issues in the left-hand column. The final version of the local contract should be subject to legal scrutiny and advice locally before it is used.

When commissioning intermediate care from a independent sector provider (in a residential setting), you should refer to the *Care homes for older people. National minimum standards* (Department of Health, 2002e). Standard 6 relates specifically to intermediate care, and most of the other standards will also be relevant.

Standard 6 Intermediate care

Outcome: service users assessed and referred solely for intermediate care are helped to maximise their independence and return home.

6.1   Where service users are admitted only for intermediate care, dedicated accommodation is provided, together with specialised facilities, equipment and staff, to deliver short term intensive rehabilitation and enable service users to return home.

6.2   Rehabilitation facilities are sited in dedicated space and include equipment for therapies and treatment, as well as equipment to promote activities of daily living and mobility.

6.3   Staff are qualified and/or are trained and appropriately supervised to use techniques for rehabilitation including treatment and recovery programmes, promotion of mobility, continence and self-care, and outreach programmes to re-establish community living

6.4   Staff are deployed, and specialist services from relevant professions, including occupational and physiotherapists, are provided or secured in sufficient numbers and with sufficient competence and skills to meet the assessed needs of service users admitted for rehabilitation.

6.5 The service user placed for intermediate care is not admitted for long term care unless and until the requirements regarding information, assessment and care planning (Standards 1, 3 and 7) are met.

Department of Health (2002e). *Care homes for older people. National minimum standards (Care Standards Act 2000)*. London: Department of Health.

The voluntary sector has the potential to contribute to individual support of this type. For example, Age Concern England is running a number of pilot schemes in which volunteers carry out social rehabilitation as part of the overall package of care provided to a client. The Red Cross also supports a number of hospital discharge schemes (*see* Further reading, p. 89).

The Winter and Emergency Services Team (WEST) held a workshop at the National Winter Planning Conference in May 2000 to explore the potential problems of working with the independent sector and how to solve them. The findings are shown in Table 3 (below).

TABLE 3: INTERMEDIATE CARE AND WORKING WITH THE INDEPENDENT SECTOR

This workshop gave participants views from a practitioner on practical, clinical governance and quality issues and contained a general discussion on the involvement of the independent sector.

POTENTIAL PROBLEMS	POTENTIAL WAYS OF ADDRESSING THE PROBLEMS
Use of independent sector to provide intermediate care services may destabilise the market in some areas.	Consider as part of whole system and make an impact analysis.
Lack of skills to commission from independent sector to arrive at cost effective, appropriate services with available capacity.	Draw on local government experience. Involve the independent sector in whole system discussions and develop longer-term relationships. (Don't use them one month, and drop them the next.)
Charging distortions, separate budgets, and organisational boundaries.	Pool budgets with clear guidance and shared ownership.
Old-fashioned patient and carer expectations when it comes to alternatives to hospitals, discharge from hospitals, and discharge from intermediate care.	Make the service expectations clear at the outset, but underestimate the likely length of stay. (It is easier to extend the stay of someone who expects to be in for a few days than to shorten the stay of someone who expects to be in for two weeks.) Develop public education/ understanding. 'Contract' with patients and carers.
Difficulties in identifying the right service to meet need.	Have a spectrum of services but a single point of contact and a single assessment tool. Undertake cross-sector and inter-profession training.
Issues of professional and public confidence.	Develop risk management strategies alongside clear accountabilities. Over-manage the risks at the outset of a new service to establish confidence and credibility. (Ease up later.)
Uncertain models of management.	PCGs/PCTs and their capacity to lead? Make joined-up commissioning real.
Funding is uni-agency, fragmented, managed by conflicting interests and has perverse incentives.	Pooled budgets? Earmarked funds? Joint responsibility? Resolve charging issues.
Stop-go short term funding.	Give consistent messages that stable funding is required longer term.
Organisational structures and barriers are not conducive to change or the delivery of seamless services.	Single organisation to lead? Role of PCTs?
Services are fragmented.	Integrate 'projects' into coherent services: aim for them to become mainstream and part of Joint Improvement Plans

Adapted from findings of the Winter and Emergency Services Team (WEST) Workshop 5, April 10, 2002

Publicising local services

New services or patterns of care take a while to become embedded in local service systems. For example, some of the rehabilitation services originally set up to relieve winter pressures were used much more in their second winter. A number of teams have reported the need repeatedly to remind people who might refer clients about the aims of the service and how to access it.

In Rotherham, the co-ordinator of the CARATs intermediate care service produced a widely circulated diagram to show staff which intermediate care opportunities are on offer, where they are based and what needs each can meet (Figure 13, below).

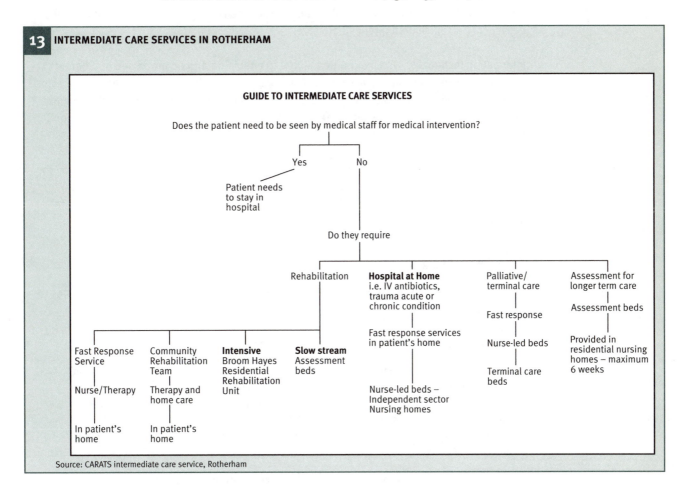

13 **INTERMEDIATE CARE SERVICES IN ROTHERHAM**

GUIDE TO INTERMEDIATE CARE SERVICES

Does the patient need to be seen by medical staff for medical intervention?

Yes — Patient needs to stay in hospital

No — Do they require

Rehabilitation:
- Fast Response Service → Nurse/Therapy → In patient's home
- Community Rehabilitation Team → Therapy and home care → In patient's home
- **Intensive** Broom Hayes Residential Rehabilitation Unit
- **Slow stream** Assessment beds

Hospital at Home i.e. IV antibiotics, trauma acute or chronic condition
- Fast response services in patient's home
- Nurse-led beds – Independent sector Nursing homes

Palliative/terminal care
- Fast response
- Nurse-led beds
- Terminal care beds

Assessment for longer term care
- Assessment beds
- Provided in residential nursing homes – maximum 6 weeks

Source: CARATS intermediate care service, Rotherham

Assessment

The Government states that intermediate care should be 'provided on the basis of a comprehensive assessment' and 'involve cross-professional working, within a single assessment framework, single professional records and shared protocols' (Department of Health, 2002c).

Guidance on the single assessment process was issued in January 2002 (Department of Health, 2002c) and details of some of the available tools and scales followed in February (Department of Health, 2002d).

It is expected that the single assessment process will provide better and more efficient access to care services, supporting the drive to deliver person-centred care outlined in the National Service Framework for Older People (Department of Health, 2001b). It should save older people from having to repeat their personal details and needs to a range of different professionals.

The new process must inevitably cross boundaries – of setting, profession and agency. Relatively large numbers of people will be involved, and they must all agree on – and adhere to – new working practices if whole system changes are to happen. There will not be a single 'right way forward'. Local solutions must be worked out, taking account of existing arrangements and working practices, and ensuring local ownership and local commitment to change (Stevenson, 1999).

Since assessment is critical to the effective delivery of intermediate care, it follows that the assessment processes in the intermediate care system must, over time, draw on and add to the single record for each client. To ensure that this happens, intermediate care co-ordinators need to link into the local development process for single assessment. The timely transfer of relevant information as the individual moves through the care system is fundamental to the delivery of person-centred intermediate care.

Information technology systems can be tailored to enable data to be processed in different ways for different purposes. It may be possible to link data-gathering in the intermediate care system for individual care planning purposes with both data-gathering as part of the single assessment process and data-gathering for evaluation purposes (*see* Section 7, 'Evaluation', p. 91).

Primary care trusts may be particularly well placed to take the lead in promoting this vision for information sharing across the whole care system. This is because, since most people are registered with a GP practice, it is GPs who are the most likely participants in the system to hold individual core records.

Tools and scales

This section comprises extracts from the tools and scales guidance (Department of Health, 2002d):

Assessment tools and scales – key points

The tools and scales guidance does not recommend particular tools for single assessment. There are two reasons for this. First, developers of assessment tools for national or local use are currently reviewing their tools to ensure that they comply with the single assessment process guidance. Second, useful approaches to assessment, including the generation of forms and procedures for rounded assessments of older people's needs, have been developed in some localities.

Asking these localities to replace their good local initiatives with a nationally prescribed assessment tool would damage local achievements and ownership.

When developing their approaches to overview and comprehensive assessment, localities may wish to explore the assessment tools listed below. Contact details are given for further information. Brief descriptions of each tool are also provided. These descriptions have been provided by the developers of each tool. They do not necessarily represent the views of the Department of Health.

Localities should bear in mind that none of the tools listed below currently meets the criteria for overview assessment given in the January 2002 guidance and in this guidance. (Developers are, however, aware of the progress that needs to be made.) If localities wish to use one of the listed tools for overview assessment, they will have to add to it or modify it, possibly in consultation with the developers.

Adapted from Department of Health (2002d). *The single assessment process: assessment tools and scales.* London: Department of Health.

The box below lists the tools and scales described in the above extract.

RECOMMENDED ASSESSMENT TOOLS AND SCALES

Tools for overview assessment
Camberwell Assessment for the Needs of the Elderly (CANE)
EASYcare 2002–2005
Functional Assessment of the Care Environment (FACE)
Minimum Data Set for Home Care (MDS Home Care)

Tools for comprehensive assessment in the community
Camberwell Assessment for the Needs of the Elderly (CANE)
Functional Assessment of the Care Environment (FACE)
Minimum Data Set for Home Care (MDS Home Care)
Sheffield 'Rainbow Assessment'

Tools for comprehensive assessment in care homes
Minimum Data Set – Resident Assessment Instrument
Royal College of Nursing Assessment Tool for Nursing Older People

Adapted from www.doh.gov.uk/scg/sap/toolsandscales/index.htm

Choosing an assessment tool

The tools that you use either for overview or comprehensive assessment should be consistent with the guidance given by the Department of Health (2002d), particularly Annex C.

In essence, the guidance states that the tool used should:

- make explicit the contribution older people make to their assessment
- bring to the fore the views, wishes, strengths and abilities of older people
- show the impact of environments, relationships and other external factors on the needs of older people
- support professional judgement rather than replacing it
- employ scales that are valid, reliable and culturally sensitive, and do not unfairly discriminate against people on the grounds of age, gender, race, disability and other factors
- help professionals both to link different parts of the assessment and to evaluate risks. It should suggest further assessment where appropriate
- adequately cover all the domains and subdomains of the single assessment process
- be suitable for use by health and social care professionals. It should be made clear whether specific skills or qualifications are required to administer the tool.

Whatever the tools used, bear in mind that assessment is only the first stage in the process of providing support. It should provide the information you need to develop care plans that help users achieve their personal goals (Department of Health, 1998a).

Take into account the views and aspirations of older people and their carers. Professionals who can gain access to the services and support that will meet the user's needs must be involved with them in making decisions about care plans and subsequent reviews.

A set of benchmarks for assessment practice has been proposed (Nolan and Caldock, 1996):

Benchmarks for assessment practice

A good assessor will:

1. Empower both the user and carer – inform fully, clarify their understanding of the situation and of the role of the assessor before going ahead.
2. Involve, rather than just inform, the user and carer – make them feel that they are a full partner in the assessment.
3. Shed their 'professional' perspective – have an open mind and be prepared to learn.
4. Start from where the user and carer are – establish their existing level of knowledge and what hopes and expectations they have.
5. Be interested in the user and carer as people.
6. Establish a suitable environment for the assessment, which ensures there is privacy, quiet and sufficient time.
7. Take time – build trust and rapport, and overcome the 'brief visitor' syndrome. This will usually take more than one visit.
8. Be sensitive, imaginative and creative in responding – users and carers may not know what is possible or available. For carers in particular, guilt and reticence may have to be overcome.
9. Avoid value judgements whenever possible – if such judgements are needed, make them explicit.
10. Consider social, emotional and relationship needs, as well as just practical needs and difficulties. Pay particular attention to the quality of the relationship between user and carer.
11. Listen to and value the user's and carer's expertise or opinions, even if these run counter to the assessor's own values.
12. Present honest, realistic service options, identifying advantages and disadvantages and providing an indication of any delay or limitations in service delivery.
13. Not make assessment a 'battle' in which users and carers feel they have to fight for services.
14. Balance all perspectives.
15. Clarify understanding at the end of the assessment, agree objectives and the nature of the review process.

Adapted from Nolan M and Caldock K (1996). Assessment: identifying the barriers to good practice. *Health and Social Care in the Community* 4(2): 77–85.

Ideally, the information collected during assessment should be useful to a variety of people, since complex needs require health and local authority interventions. The assessment should cover the domains appropriate for intervention by each of the agencies providing services, and should lead to the identification of the same needs whichever professional undertakes it and wherever it takes place (Carpenter, 1998). In order to provide the best care, an assessor must be able to identify problems that lie within the domain of another professional.

Teams that have built trust among their members and developed a shared understanding of their members' roles and skills have been successful in sharing assessment information and working together to construct a process for individual care planning and review. The single assessment process guidance requires this approach to be extended across the care system.

The role of the intermediate care co-ordinator

The Department of Health guidance (2001a) on intermediate care advises 'the NHS and councils to appoint jointly an intermediate care co-ordinator in each Health Authority area initially'. And in the National Service Framework for Older People, one of the first milestones is that 'local health and social care systems are to have designated a jointly appointed intermediate care co-ordinator in at least each health authority area' by July 2001 (Department of Health, 2001b).

In 2001, the King's Fund and the Department of Health organised two workshops to clarify the role of the intermediate care co-ordinator. A consensus emerged that co-ordination must be carried out at both strategic and operational level in care communities. In complex communities, however, it was felt that one person would not be able to manage both tasks.

The King's Fund subsequently published a briefing paper (Wilson and Stevenson, 2001) listing:

> ... the functions and tasks to be carried out in each care community to ensure an effective and efficient intermediate care system. Some are clearly strategic, and as such could be entrusted to a strategic level planning group and/or one senior individual. Many are clearly operational tasks, however, and will require close day-to-day management to ensure a high-quality and efficient programme of care for patients.
>
> Wilson K and Stevenson J (2001). *Intermediate care co-ordination: the function.* London: King's Fund.

How these functions and tasks are managed will depend very much on which services already exist locally, how far they are integrated, and the numbers, skills and experience of staff. In areas of high organisational complexity, a number of people may be needed to ensure that all the tasks are carried out. In relatively simple systems, one person may be able to perform them all.

How responsibility is allocated will depend upon a number of factors at local level. These will include:

- the size, demography, complexity and maturity of the local health and social care systems and associated intermediate care system.
- the skills, experience and capacity of the individuals available to ensure that the function of co-ordination is carried out.
- the local style of management, in terms of how management roles generally combine or separate operational and strategic roles.

> Local systems will have to decide how much of the full spectrum of tasks is included in the role of the local co-ordinator – this will need to fit local arrangements overall.
>
> Wilson and Stevenson (2001), as above.

Where the role of the co-ordinator is clearly focused on operational functions only, you will need to make arrangements for the strategic function to be discharged by another person or persons. However, you should also ensure that the co-ordinator has a major advisory input into the strategic process.

In some circumstances, the co-ordinator will be responsible for the operational function together with some, but not all, aspects of strategy. In such cases, it is important to make clear with whom the overall responsibility for strategic intermediate care development rests.

> Specific roles and areas of responsibility/accountability will all need to be stated clearly in job descriptions, which will therefore vary according to local arrangements.
>
> Wilson and Stevenson (2001), as above.

The context for strategic development

Responsibility for the strategic development of intermediate care will rest with the NSF Local Implementation Team.

Overall responsibility for implementing intermediate care as an NSF standard will rest with the chief officer who has the local mandate for co-ordinating NSF implementation.

The NSF implies that each standard should itself be led by a nominated local chief officer; by implication, this includes intermediate care.

Local implementation plans, including those for intermediate care, will be part of the annual Joint Investment Plan, alongside other plans for services for older people.

> @
> Available at:
> www.doh.gov.uk/
> cebulletin11april.htm#1

From 2002–03, the NHS will no longer be required to produce either older people's or intermediate care Joint Investment Plans. Instead, chief executives of the new strategic health authorities will outline the actions and investments required to deliver intermediate care (and other priorities) in Annual Delivery Agreements (ADAs) with the Department of Health. @

Strategic and operational level functions

The following two extracts comprise detailed descriptions of strategic and operational level functions, adapted from Wilson and Stevenson (2001):

Strategic level functions

Purpose
to ensure that intermediate care is integrated across the statutory and independent sectors and across primary care, community health services, social care, housing and the acute sector.

Tasks
Service planning and development
- to ensure that service planning for intermediate care takes place within the context of service planning for the NSF generally, and within the JIP process
- to develop service models, or change working practices, to improve the quality of existing services or to meet unmet need for intermediate care
- to secure local agreement on the provision of medical services, and monitoring of standards, in support of intermediate care provided in the statutory and independent sector.

Delivering integrated care
- to ensure that arrangements exist to provide a consistent and integrated response across the whole system of health and social care in the designated area
- to map existing intermediate care provision, and to check that criteria, transfer protocols and care pathways exist and are agreed by local stakeholders
- to liaise with stakeholders in neighbouring localities to ensure the effective management of cross-boundary patient flow in respect of intermediate care.

Finances
- to ensure that financial resources for intermediate care services are clearly identified and supported with efficient systems of financial management
- to develop shared/pooled budgets for intermediate care across health and social services.

Workforce
- to ensure that explicit arrangements and clear lines of accountability exist for the management of case managers and other staff involved in the provision of intermediate care across the whole system.

Information and communications
- to develop joint protocols and decision-making and information-sharing processes within the area, across professional and organisational boundaries, where these are not yet agreed, with particular emphasis on links with mainstream services
- to gather information from a wide network on research and innovation in intermediate care, and act as an expert point of reference for commissioners and service providers locally
- to ensure that developments in intermediate care are effectively communicated to local stakeholder organisations, staff and the public.

Evaluation
- to ensure that arrangements exist for monitoring, auditing and evaluating the quality and effectiveness of intermediate care
- to develop data systems and evaluation measures to provide information on service performance/trends and to identify gaps and outcomes for individuals
- to evaluate the overall effectiveness of the intermediate care system, and the services within it, against agreed performance criteria.

Operational level functions

Purpose
to optimise the quality of care for individual service users by ensuring oversight and efficient management of intermediate care in a defined locality on behalf of the commissioning agencies.

Tasks
Care of individuals
- identifying clients who would benefit from intermediate care and ensuring their smooth transfer in accordance with an agreed care plan
- making plans prior to admission for elective patients admitted to acute hospital care with an anticipated discharge pathway through intermediate care
- making plans for non-elective patients as soon as they are transferred
- monitoring progress against care plans, ensuring that care is available as agreed and that clients achieve their personal outcomes
- ensuring clinical and social care input to assessment, as well as client involvement and carer involvement where this is appropriate and in keeping with the client's wishes
- making sure that clients enter services at the most appropriate point on an agreed care pathway, with a named case manager and individual care plan and review date, building on local assessment and care management arrangements
- ensuring that equipment needs are identified and swiftly met, and that equipment is retrieved when a client no longer needs it
- ensuring that systems exist to trigger other actions whilst the client is in intermediate care, for example: home adaptations, putting together domiciliary care packages.

Access to services
- reviewing and developing clear admission criteria for each scheme within the locality and ensuring that there is no duplication
- promoting awareness of the intermediate care system, admission criteria and access point(s) among potential referrers
- agreeing access to intermediate care out of office and at weekends (e.g. via GP co-ops) with key partners and service providers
- helping GPs and other referrers to locate the most appropriate service, by problem solving and directing clients on the threshold of inappropriate hospital admission to the most appropriate level of care
- either negotiating placements into and discharges out of intermediate care, or authorising patient transfers arranged by appropriately designated case managers.

Commissioning/contracting
- ensuring that appropriate service specifications exist for all intermediate care settings.

- monitoring intermediate care services to ensure contract compliance in all aspects of care and capacity to provide high-quality care appropriate to client needs
- ensuring that appropriate medical cover is arranged via either a GP or a hospital specialist, in accordance with arrangements established by the commissioners of intermediate care
- ensuring that hospital consultants other than those specialising in old age are engaged in the intermediate care system and are able to refer people to more appropriate settings.

Monitoring and evaluation
- undertaking regular planned reviews of client outcomes for each intermediate care setting
- regularly reporting data on capacity, throughput and outcomes to the commissioner
- instigating and co-ordinating audit of intermediate care services
- identifying training needs of intermediate care staff and finding ways to meet these needs
- monitoring costs of services
- setting up systems to ensure day-to-day monitoring of capacity in the intermediate care system, to ensure that clients are transferred as soon as they are ready to go to their next planned destination (maximising capacity).

Communications
- providing advice to the NSF Local Implementation Team on the strategic development of intermediate care services.

Troubleshooting
- managing a budget for problem solving
- identifying and speedily resolving problems and blockages in the system in order to ensure that other services can operate efficiently
- ensuring that agreed systems exist for the client's records/care plans to be transferred through the system with them.

Adapted from Wilson K and Stevenson J (2001). *Intermediate care co-ordination: the function.* London: King's Fund.

Responsibilities

The South West Region (the former South West Regional Office, or SWRO) compiled a list of commissioning and service delivery responsibilities included in the role of intermediate care co-ordinators:

What needs co-ordinating?

Commissioning activity
- primary care trust/social services department lead
- strategic view of needs/total bed and service requirements
- range of services/mixture
- investment priorities
- application of health authority flexibilities
- contracting methods
- comparative evaluation.

Service delivery responsibilities
- promoting understanding and knowledge of local intermediate care and equipment services
- supporting the development of integrated care pathways
- acting as a single point of access
- working with and supporting partner agencies (trusts, social service departments, Independent Sector) in delivering integrated services
- designing protocols/criteria for access to local services
- identifying needs/gaps/duplication in local provision
- management of pooled budgets

- working with partner agencies to ensure integration of service delivery across primary and secondary care, community health service, social care, housing/repairs/adaptation, independent sector
- monitoring take-up, trends, quality and appropriateness of referral
- evaluation and audit
- contributing to training, education and local workforce planning arrangements
- working closely to develop strong links with the new arrangements for a single assessment process and local care management.

SWRO, internal documentation

In conclusion, note that two specific challenges face intermediate care co-ordinators:

Organisational change in care communities (for example, developments in strategic health authorities and primary care trusts) may in turn necessitate changes in the way that intermediate care is co-ordinated.

The focus on co-ordination of the current service system must not be allowed to inhibit the identification of further opportunities to develop new service responses or change current working practices and the way resources are currently used.

Adapted from Wilson K and Stevenson J (2001). *Intermediate care co-ordination: the function.* London: King's Fund.

 Key points from this section

- **Strong leadership is essential for intermediate care development.**
- **Engage the support of existing staff for your plans; the literature on the management of change will be helpful here.**
- **Look at the potential for new ways of working by health care teams, rehabilitation teams and rehabilitation assistants.**
- **Arrange for medical input into the new services.**
- **Look at patient pathways to ensure that the new services are flexible enough to meet the needs of all users and ensure continuity of care.**
- **If appropriate, contract out some services to the independent sector.**
- **Agree upon a single assessment process with all stakeholders; use tools and scales that meet Department of Health criteria.**
- **Look at how the new services will be co-ordinated and what specific tasks will be involved.**

 # Further reading

Audit Commission (2001). *Change here! Managing change to improve local services.* London: Audit Commission.

Burke S and Neilson E (2002). *Pharmacists and the new intermediate care agenda.* London: Royal Pharmaceutical Society of Great Britain.

Department of Health and Public Services Productivity Panel (2000). *Working in partnership: developing a whole systems approach.* Leeds: NHS Executive. Available at: www.doh.gov.uk/ipu/pspp/partner.htm

Department of Health/Royal College of General Practitioners (2002). *Guidelines for the appointment of general practitioners with special interests: framework.* Available at: www.doh.gov.uk/pricare/gp-specialinterests/index.htm

Department of Health/Royal College of General Practitioners (2002). *Guidelines for the appointment of general practitioners with special interests in the delivery of clinical services: intermediate and continuing care for older people.* Available at: www.doh.gov.uk/pricare/gp-specialinterests/gpwsioldercare.pdf

Department of Health/Royal College of General Practitioners (2002). *Guidelines for the appointment of general practitioners with special interests in the role of service development: primary care coronary heart disease lead.* Available at: www.doh.gov.uk/pricare/gp-specialinterests/gpwsiservdevchd.pdf

Department of Health/Royal College of General Practitioners (2002). *Implementing a scheme for general practitioners with special interests.* Available at: www.doh.gov.uk/pricare/gp-specialinterests/gpwsiframework.pdf

Foote C and Stanners C (2002). *Integrating services for older people.* London: Jessica Kingsley Publishers.

Hall, J (2000). A partnership between British Red Cross and rehabilitation services in South Cheshire. *Rehabilitation Development Network News Update* 5: 10. London: King's Fund.

Howden J (2002). The South Staffordshire Intermediate Care Training and Development Project. *British Journal of Occupational Therapy* 65(3): 138–40.

Institute of Medicine (2001). *Crossing the quality chasm: a new health system for the 21st century.* Washington DC: National Academy Press.

McCormack B (2001). *Autonomy and the relationship between nurses and older people.* Ageing and Society 21(4): 417–45.

McGrath H, George J and Young J (2002). The rehabilitation of older people from ethnic minorities, in Squires A and Hastings M (eds) *Rehabilitation of the older person: a handbook for the multidisciplinary team.* 3rd edition. Cheltenham: Nelson Thornes.

NHS Modernisation Agency (2002). *Improvement leaders' guide to process, mapping, analysis and redesign*, available at: www.modern.nhs.uk/improvementguides/process/

Office for Public Management (2001). *The joint appointments guide: a guide to setting up, managing and maintaining joint appointments for health improvement between health organisations and local government.* OPM, London.

Ormiston H (2002). The single assessment process. *MCC: Building knowledge for integrated care* (10) 2: 38–43.

Vaughan B, Steiner A and Hanford L (1999). *Intermediate care: the shape of the team.* London: King's Fund.

7 Evaluation

The NHS and local authorities are charged with ensuring that intermediate care is suitably evaluated and that systems for evaluation are built into new intermediate care arrangements at the earliest possible stage. This section will show you how to develop a simple framework for evaluating intermediate care. The framework can also be used as a quality improvement tool if it is designed as part of a continuous quality improvement process.

This section will look at:
- why it is important to evaluate
- developing an evaluation framework
- when to establish a framework
- which model to use.

Why it is important to evaluate

The Government has high expectations of intermediate care to:

- promote independence and improve the quality of life of older people
- solve system pressures in the acute hospital sector.

It is therefore very important that you should be able to demonstrate the outcomes of providing new services, reconfiguring services or changing working practices. Many of the early innovators in intermediate care found that their data collection systems were inadequate for this task.

Early initiatives, such as residential rehabilitation schemes and rapid response teams, were often set up very quickly, in response to new short-term funding received at short notice, for example, to address winter pressures. Little time was given to devising explicit statements of service aims or deciding how outcomes would be monitored and evaluated.

Many staff subsequently found that the data they could retrieve with difficulty would not answer the various questions about effectiveness posed by the different stakeholders in the care system. For example, data showing that the physical function of service users had improved over time was of little comfort to chief executives who had failed to meet targets to reduce delayed discharges. Individual longer-term outcomes were rarely considered.

Developing an evaluation framework

Almost by definition, intermediate care services have direct implications for a range of sectors along the health and social care continuum (Steiner *et al.*, 1998). Any evaluation framework must be robust enough to accommodate the complexity of intermediate care provision. It must cover the person receiving care, their carers and their family, as well as the practitioners involved and the agencies responsible. Commissioners of services will also be interested in the results.

The evaluation process must address the needs and preferences of stakeholders. This means tackling the issues that are important to them and expressing the results in a format they will understand. For example, both health and social care staff are likely to be involved. Traditionally, they have expressed themselves in different ways: health staff often use quantitative methods ('counting'), social services staff often use qualitative methods ('describing').

You should include both approaches to accommodate the two different perspectives. Acknowledging this diversity will enrich the evaluation process, as well as helping to ensure the commitment of all stakeholders to the results and any changes subsequently required.

When to establish a framework

Ideally, you should agree on a framework for evaluation before a new service begins, or before making changes to existing provision. When setting up the evaluation, you must identify indicators, measures and benchmarks against which the outcomes of the new services or changes can be assessed. (If benchmarks are not available, the initial evaluation may set the baseline.) This is especially important if the changes are expected to have an effect on other parts of the current service system. Having an evaluation process will thus further refine the purpose and design of new care processes: a 'virtuous circle'.

Which model to use

We have chosen to describe an evaluation model based on the 'balanced scorecard' method first developed in the USA and later refined in Sweden and elsewhere (Kaplan and Norton, 1992; Olve *et al.*, 1999). This method is much less complex than other models, such as the value compass (Cox *et al.*, 1999). It involves monitoring a range of dimensions within the same time frame. The reporting system thus gives a complete picture at given points in time, reflecting not only the complexity of intermediate care, but also a whole systems approach.

The rationale behind this method is that change in any of the areas being monitored is likely to affect the rest of the system in some way and this needs to be recognised. Discussion with all stakeholders will help to increase understanding of the system and its complexities, and should identify any potential for change.

According to this model, the service to be evaluated is monitored in four key areas:

- client experience/satisfaction
- care outcome
- process
- cost effectiveness.

For each key area, the people responsible for the evaluation must agree on:

- a range of indicators or measures
- what information will be collected, and how
- who will routinely check performance using each of these measures.

Appendix 7 (p. 119) shows how Merton, Sutton and Wandsworth Health Authority developed an evaluation framework, outlining what data will be collected and by whom. Based on this, Merton and Sutton Primary Care Trust developed a data collection proforma, shown in Appendix 8 (p. 121). This is currently being piloted in scannable format for ease of analysis.

The data collected must be analysed in relation to the expected outcomes, also taking into account the principles and values of the service. Where complex and technical issues are concerned, you may need skilled external evaluators.

You will need to involve people likely to be affected by the proposed changes at the design stage. If they are not involved early on, they may not accept the evaluation and may reject any changes that the evaluation suggests are needed. The effects of change are usually said to be felt up to two levels away in each direction from the area being evaluated – therefore you must involve people from all these levels.

For example, when deciding how to evaluate intermediate care that aims to avoid unnecessary admission through the A&E department, you should involve staff from the older people's rehabilitation ward, as well as staff from the A&E department, local authority care home, independent sector residential/nursing home and primary care team, and any local older people who have used the services.

A list of areas to evaluate, together with examples of tools and measures that can be used to do this, is given in Figure 14 (below). Table 4 (overleaf) provides additional examples of tools and measures. Figure 15 (p. 95) shows diagrammatically how this approach can be built into a cycle of continuous evaluation and improvement (Foote and Stanners, 2002).

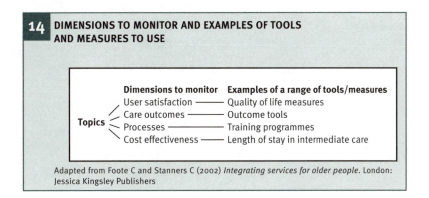

14 DIMENSIONS TO MONITOR AND EXAMPLES OF TOOLS AND MEASURES TO USE

Dimensions to monitor	Examples of a range of tools/measures
User satisfaction	Quality of life measures
Care outcomes	Outcome tools
Processes	Training programmes
Cost effectiveness	Length of stay in intermediate care

Topics

Adapted from Foote C and Stanners C (2002) *Integrating services for older people.* London: Jessica Kingsley Publishers

TABLE 4: TOPIC AREAS AND TOOLS/MEASURES FOR EVALUATING INTERMEDIATE CARE

USER SATISFACTION	CARE OUTCOMES	PROCESSES	COST-EFFECTIVENESS
Patient/user/carer questionnaires Quality of life measures: ■ SF36* ■ EQ-5D ■ PDQ 39 (specific to Parkinson's disease) COPE (carers' satisfaction) Achievement of jointly agreed personal goals: ■ Canadian Occupational Performance Measure* ■ TELER (Treatment and Evaluation of Le Roy Scale)* ■ Goal Attainment (Achievement) Scale* Complaints	Goal achievement scales Assessment tools/outcome measures: ■ Barthel Index ■ Abbreviated Mental Test Score ■ HONOS ■ Cape (Clifton Assessment Procedures for the Elderly) ■ Carer Strain Index ■ Elderly Mobility Scale ■ Assessment and Motor Performance Scale ■ FIM (Functional Independence Measure) ■ FAM (Functional Assessment Measure) ■ GDS (Geriatric Depression Scale) ■ Hospital Anxiety and Depression Scale ■ IADL (Index of Independence in Activities of Daily Living) ■ Nottingham Extended ADL Scale ■ REPDS (Revised Elderly Persons Disability Scale) ■ Rivermead Mobility Index ■ TOMS (Therapy Outcome Measure Scale) ■ Waterlow Assessment. Theories of change Reduction in delayed transfers† Inappropriate admissions† Inappropriate readmissions† Admission rates to long-term care† Premature admissions to long-term care† Reduction in community care packages to individuals†	Clear criteria for admission for intermediate care services/settings Care planning includes personal goal setting Information/publicity to enable appropriate referrals Referral rates/routes Staffing levels/skill mix Training programmes, eg: ■ rehabilitation approach/focus ■ risk management in the community ■ ethnic issues ■ team development Early case-finding and proactive case management Single point of access System for sharing client information across the care system (link to single assessment process) Clear arrangements for managing interfaces between services/settings Critical incident techniques	(Few examples of measures available; few agreed benchmarks) Length of stay in all intermediate care settings: ■ in general ■ by specific diagnosis/other categories Length of stay in acute beds ■ intermediate care clients ■ other specified groups Decrease in inappropriate emergency decisions Reduction in delayed transfers Prevention/health promotion, e.g. by early case finding Management of chronic care at home

Key
* Can also be categorised in **care outcomes**
† Can also be categorised in **cost-effectiveness**

NB Please note this is not an exhaustive list.

Source: King's Fund 2002

15 THE CONTINUOUS EVALUATION PROCESS

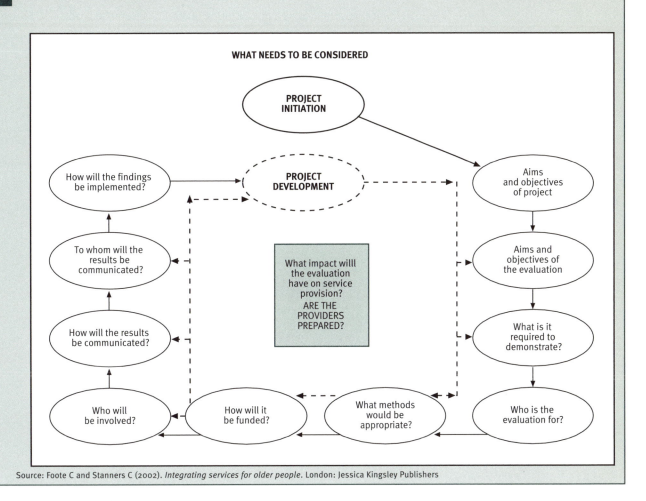

WHAT NEEDS TO BE CONSIDERED

Source: Foote C and Stanners C (2002). *Integrating services for older people*. London: Jessica Kingsley Publishers

---

→ Key points from this section

- Agree on the service(s) to be evaluated, together with the time frame.
- Identify all the stakeholders who have an interest and involve them directly.
- Select the dimensions from the balanced scorecard that will give the best whole systems appreciation of the service(s) and indicate any necessary changes.
- Select the appropriate measurement tools.
- Review the analysis procedures.
- Decide on the reporting procedures, specifying both how and to whom the results will be made available.
- Decide on the procedures to be used to make any changes identified as necessary by the evaluation.
- Start the evaluation.

Further reading

Franks A (2001). Clinical governance as a restructuring of quality assurance processes. *British Journal of Clinical Governance* (6) 4: 259–63.

Institute of Medicine (2001). *Crossing the quality chasm: a new health system for the 21st century*: 61–88. Washington DC: National Academy Press.

Keith R (1998). Patient satisfaction and rehabilitation services, *Archives of Physical Medicine and Rehabilitation* 79, no. 9: 1122–28.

NHS Modernisation Agency (2002). *Improvement leaders' guide to measurement for improvement*, available at: www.modern.nhs.uk/improvementguides/measurement/home.htm

Robinson L and Drinkwater C (June 2000). A significant case audit of a community-based resource team – an opportunity for multidisciplinary teams to introduce clinical governance? *Journal of Clinical Governance* 8: 89–96.

Appendices

Appendix 1 Developing intermediate care – initial diagnostic   99

Appendix 2 The Sheffield definition of functions of rehabilitation   103

Appendix 3 Intermediate care – classification of terms   106

Appendix 4 Models of intermediate care that aim to prevent
            hospital admissions   110

Appendix 5 Practical guidance on using health act flexibilities –
            a checklist   112

Appendix 6 Department of Health success factors for developing
            intermediate care   116

Appendix 7 Intermediate care evaluation framework   119

Appendix 8 Intermediate care evaluation data collection proforma   121

Bibliography   123

Index   130

Acknowledgements   00

QUESTIONS	SUPPLEMENTARY QUESTIONS	COMMENTS
Strategic issues		
1. Has an analysis of current demand for hospital and long-term care services been undertaken?	■ Is there understanding of what is driving demand? ■ Has analysis been undertaken by primary care group (PCG) population to produce comparative data? ■ Are particular GP practices or local social services (SS) teams showing up as 'outliers'? ■ What follow-up work has been undertaken?	
2. What are the top 10 conditions for admissions in the over 75s?	■ These are likely to be around respiratory, heart disease, falls. ■ Aware of conditions and reasons? Does planning demonstrate where efforts should be concentrated, e.g. new services for particular conditions (eg COPD or DVT or new services to target particular geographical patches)?	
3. The main reasons for 'community' referrals to long-term care?	■ Likely to be incontinence, mental health, deteriorating physical health, carers unable to cope.	
4. What is the balance of LTC placements originating from: (i) hospital (ii) community?	■ Are one or the other routes more robust regarding rigorous assessment, consideration of alternatives, gate-keeping, etc.?	
5. Are protocols in place/under development for appropriate place of care and responsibility? Right time/right place?	■ Which pathways have been developed? ■ Are there admission criteria for different conditions?	
6. Are discharge agreements in place including target times for assessment and commencement of care packages? Mental health aspects?	■ Have these been reviewed e.g. *'Better Care: Higher Standards'*? ■ Do the agreements include protocols for early commencement of assessment from point of admission? Input from MDT to A&E and MAU? ■ What are the reasons for bottlenecks in the assessment process? How this is being addressed? ■ 24-hour availability and weekends? ■ Are dispute resolution procedures in place?	Add in example target times. e.g. response to a referral – one working day – in hospital, initial assessment – two working days – in hospital and equivalent for community.
7. What is the system for managing and co-ordinating discharge?	■ Has a named person or team been identified to manage the discharge process? ■ Do wards, including A&E and MAU, consider possible treatment outcomes and discharge needs from an early point?	
8. Are Continuing Care agreements in place?	■ Do these include any further recent review? ■ Are all the elements properly addressed (assessment specialist advice, rehabilitation palliative care, transport)? ■ When were they last reviewed?	
9. Are there agreed ceilings for maximum number of delayed transfers?	Have these targets been broken down by key cause, eg: ■ assessment ■ NHS Transfer ■ funding ■ placement availability Are ceilings being reviewed/lowered each year?	
10. Are national definitions used for monitoring delayed transfers (transfer delays) as described in CIC and SITREP?	■ Attention needs to be given to wording: 'a person occupying an acute hospital bed and medically fit for discharge' (this should include input from a multi-disciplinary team). ■ Is there an estimate of length of delays/bed days lost?	
11. Are there patients or carers refusing to be discharged?	What attempts have been made to move people on? (See separate guidance.)	

QUESTIONS	SUPPLEMENTARY QUESTIONS	COMMENTS
Strategic issues		
12. How is an understanding of 'Direction on Choice' demonstrated?	■ Interpretation agreed between NHS and SSD? ■ Advice given to front line professionals?	
13. How is the independent sector actively engaged in service planning? Are there examples of short-term use of beds, e.g.: ■ to avoid admissions ■ post discharge care/recovery? How are these funded?	What are current issues? E.g.: ■ capacity ■ home closures ■ specialist care (EMI) ■ costs/local authority fee managing ■ priority to self-fundees ■ interest in rehab/intermediate care agenda.	
14. Is the contribution of housing agencies fully recognised?	■ Are there 'move-on' arrangements from residential care, e.g. to sheltered housing? ■ What unused capacity exists? ■ Have discussions taken place for the provision of extra sheltered housing and similar?	
15. Is there a named responsible officer charged with reporting on discharge delays? Are readmission rates being monitored?	■ Is full use made of CIC data and trends in SITREP? ■ Which groups receive reports? ■ What arrangements are in place for audit to trace cause and take rectifying action?	
16. Have use of special grants, identified funds or growth money, intended to promote independence/care closer to home, been reviewed?	■ Are projects being managed to ensure targets/target groups benefit? ■ Are managers familiar with the evidence base on effectiveness in: – improving discharge performance – ensuring appropriate admissions?	
17. Is a communications strategy in place?	Is information from RO/HA reaching all relevant staff?	
18. How are users and carers involved in service planning and monitoring?	■ Have any patient surveys been completed? ■ Has a patient champion role been established?	
19. Are plans in place to establish joint commissioning for Older People's services?		
20. Are local leadership (council member or non-executive) practice champion for older people's services established?		
21. Are ward facilities adequate?	■ Do OP wards have rehabilitation facilities close by? ■ Are all OP wards single sex? ■ Nightingale or bay design? ■ If not, are plans in place for service by 2004 following RCP guidelines?	
OPERATIONAL ISSUES		
22. Is a medical assessment unit established?	■ Number of beds? ■ Adequately staffed? ■ Emphasis on assessment rather than admissions?	
23. Has the MAU access to rapid assessment facilities?	■ 24 hrs/7 day available? ■ What links exist with A&E? – i.e. multi-disciplinary within 72 hours or other locally determined time target (specify)?	
24. Are special arrangements put in place for rapid transfer of patients home?	■ Are support arrangements for nursing, personal care easily and quickly accessible to cope with short-term needs including the use of the voluntary sector? ■ 24 hour/7 day? ■ Proper arrangements for coordination, e.g. named nurse? ■ Transport?	

QUESTIONS	SUPPLEMENTARY QUESTIONS	COMMENTS
OPERATIONAL ISSUES		
25. Are services sufficiently flexible to meet fluctuating demands?	■ 24 hr/7 days available? ■ When/where are the peaks – time of day/day of week/month/by referer?	
26. What is the number of rehabilitation beds? Is the therapy input available adequate: ■ in hospital ■ in community – short term up to 6–8 weeks?	■ 7 day available? ■ What level of therapy input on average, e.g. 10 minutes per day (Audit Commission benchmark)? ■ Types of therapy available?	
27. Is there primary care rapid access to: ■ diagnostic services ■ consultant opinion ■ multidisciplinary assessment ■ intermediate care beds ■ triage?	■ 24 hour/7 days?	
28. What services are in place to: ■ prevent avoidable admissions ■ facilitate timely discharge ■ minimise premature admission to long-term care?	■ 24 hr/7 days available?	
29. How do pre-admission arrangements for elective patients initiate discharge planning?	■ Is there follow through the system to flag up in acute wards? ■ 24 hour/7 days available?	
30. Is literature available to patients and carers to explain admission, assessment and discharge procedures?	■ Are there back-up arrangements if community CMs are absent/unavailable?	
31. What steps have been taken to ensure residential and nursing homes have advice and support to prevent avoidable hospital admissions?	■ Have discussions taken place to agree protocols for appropriate admissions? ■ What primary care medical/nursing/therapy support is available – what has been agreed? ■ Is there a process for reviewing appropriateness of LTC placements? ■ 24 hr/7 days available?	
32. Has a joint equipment store been established with agreed access for routine aids and equipment including a single assessment process?	■ Arrangements in place/planned for 24 hour and 7 days per week access? ■ Is there a local DLC/ILC?	
33. Can health and SSD access a 'handyperson' scheme for prompt minor work?	■ What is the waiting time? ■ 24 hr/7 days available? ■ Is voluntary sector (CVS) involved in co-ordinating local voluntary effort?	
34. What is the waiting time for major home adaptations?	■ What actions have been attempted to improve this?	
35. What attempts have been made to bring together primary care and SSD out-of-hours services?		
36. Is transport available OOH/weekends/peak periods?		
37. Does a protocol exist with ambulance trusts for discharge at short notice?		

QUESTIONS	SUPPLEMENTARY QUESTIONS	COMMENTS
OPERATIONAL ISSUES		
38. Are protocols established for managing people with mental health problems within physical/ general setting?		
39. What rapid response services are available for people with mental health needs?	■ 24 hr/7 days available? ■ Is there agreement with and between providers on management and coordination?	
40. What health promotion services are established – hypothermia; diet; medication; condition specific, e.g. stroke?		
41. Is a falls service established?	■ Are all fallers referred to falls service by A&E? ■ Do GPs access falls service?	
42. What arrangements are in place/under development for risk assessment for over-75s?	■ Do all GPs offer 75+ health checks? ■ Plans to produce register of vulnerable people in conjunction with social services. ■ How are vulnerable older people identified? ■ Once identified, what assessment process takes place?	
43. How are staff training needs around behaviour and attitude identified and addressed?		
44. How are new schemes being evaluated?	■ Is evaluation in place? ■ Is evaluation available?	
45. Identify respite care services.	■ Older people ■ Older people with mental health needs	
46. How do continence services currently operate?		
47. Is a specialised stroke unit/team in place?		
NSF MILESTONES – Current position		
48. Intermediate care lead	By July 2001	
49. CES lead	By July 2001	
50. Audits of all age related policies	October 2001	
51. Baseline audit CES	October 2001	
52. JOP (including intermediate care)	By January 2001	
53. Data collection established to compare 1999/00 and 2001/02 for:- ■ Intermediate care beds ■ Intermediate care service and users ■ Intermediate care – preventing admission	March 2002	
54. The Single Assessment process is introduced	April 2002	
55. Councils to have reviewed eligibility criteria for age discrimination	April 2002	
56. MD for older people and nurse leader posts established	April 2002	
57. Plans for stroke services ■ plans prepared ■ for implementation	 April 2002 April 2004	
58. CES Draft Plan for integration and 50% increase in users by 2004	April 2002	
59. Information for users and carers reviewed	April 2002	

Adapted from the material available at: www.doh.gov.uk/swo/olderpeopleservices.htm

EIGHT PROGRAMMES OF CARE

1. Person needs prevention/maintenance programme

Aims	■ prevent physical and psychological deterioration ■ prevent loss of independence ■ promote psychological well-being ■ encourage healthy living ■ promote positive attitude to independence
Services	■ home care/support – social enablers
Setting	■ own home – local community setting
Status of person	■ slight frailty or some physical/psychological threat to independent living
Include	■ individuals with physical/emotional or cognitive disorder who will not benefit from active rehabilitation but who need monitoring and advice
Exclude	■ persons not at risk of deterioration ■ any person wishing to exercise personal responsibility for this ■ anyone receiving continuing health service where responsibility for can be identified and passed over

2. Person needs active convalescence

Aims	■ encourage improvement and/or maintenance of independence ■ improve recuperation ■ wait for aids adaptations ■ wait for family adjustment support ■ adjust to new circumstances
Services	■ home support ■ residential } not specialist ■ general care
Setting	■ step-down beds ■ own home ■ short-term residential home
Status of person	■ general malaise but generally well, most independent
Include	■ those needing encouragement, extra time, verbal support, general enablement and confidence building
Exclude	■ any person whose family are willing and able to provide convalescence ■ any person needing active rehabilitation

3. Person needs slow-stream rehabilitation

Aims	■ provide watchful waiting ■ provide assessment/observation ■ provide non-intensive rehabilitation/mobilisation ■ improve confidence ■ actively encourage, extend and facilitate increased speed of recovery ■ provide support programme, carried out by person and carers
Services	■ community rehabilitation team ■ home support } generalised/enablement skills ■ out-patient therapy
Setting	■ own home – nursing home care ■ intermediate care beds
Status of person	■ stable condition, moderate level of disability, partially dependent, potential for improvement; may have combination of disabling condition
Include	■ those with mild impairments and disabilities who need specific guidance, treatment and the opportunity to practise new approaches and techniques ■ those requiring rehabilitation with reduced stamina ■ those with slowly deteriorating conditions
Exclude	■ those more likely to benefit from another programme ■ those with stamina and ability to benefit from more active rehabilitation

NB: People may move from one category to another

4. Person needs regular rehabilitation programme

Aims	■ provide rehabilitation to maintain steady and measurable progress ■ improve expected recovery path
Services	■ community rehabilitation ■ home support
Setting	■ home, out-patients, day hospital
Status of person	■ person progressing in rehabilitation, further recovery expected ■ intensive rehabilitation not appropriately given ■ nature of person's condition and length of time since onset
Include	■ those people who can benefit from active targeted, goal-orientated treatment from a multidisciplinary team ■ those with ability to retain information, co-operate and understand rehabilitation objectives
Exclude	■ those more likely to benefit from other programmes ■ those who are not making measurable progress with regular intervention

5. Person needs intensive rehabilitation

Aims	■ change from dependence to independence ■ reduce level of dependence on carers ■ achieve maximum level of function ■ resolve acute disabling conditions
Services	■ community rehabilitation ■ home support ■ specialist therapy teams } specialist skills ■ specialised nursing
Setting	■ home ■ rehabilitation ward ■ intermediate care ■ day hospital
Status of person	■ medically very fit, motivated, but dependent, and identified by therapist as good candidate for intensive rehabilitation
Include	■ fit, motivated person with (mostly) acute condition judged able to contribute significantly to active treatment ■ person requiring intensive treatment to reinforce new skills/overcome specific impairment
Exclude	■ person who will benefit from another programme ■ person unable to tolerate level of intervention ■ person not making measurable improvement

6. Person needs specific treatment for individual acute disabling condition

Aims	■ target specific treatment by one profession ■ alleviate or reduce specific impairment/disability
Services	■ specialised therapy/nursing
Setting	■ community/domiciliary therapy ■ out-patient therapy
Status of person	■ medically stable, single acute or chronic disabling impairment which can be managed by one specific professional
Include	■ person with single defined disabling condition ■ goal be clearly defined; intensity of input may vary
Exclude	■ person with diffuse or generalised disability requiring team approach ■ person unable to contribute to therapy programme

NB: People may move from one category to another

7. Person needs medical care and rehabilitation

Aims	■ actively treat medical condition in order to prevent/modify deterioration or secondary sequelae while enabling person to improve/maintain independence ■ appropriately manage medical condition while person undergoing multidisciplinary rehabilitation
Services	■ medical care with generalised/specialised rehabilitation support ■ nursing care
Setting	■ home (less often) ■ rehabilitation ward ■ nursing home
Status of person	■ unwell/unstable medical condition, disabled specifically or generally
Include	■ people requiring specialised medical intervention as part of rehabilitation programme
Exclude	■ people too unwell/unstable to benefit from rehabilitation component

8. Person needs rehabilitation for complex, profound, disabling condition

Aims	■ provide rehabilitation as part of long-term management of condition ■ maximise level of function, prevent secondary disabling condition and improve quality of life ■ provide particular provision of services related to those with low-incidence specialised cognitive and physical disorders
Services	■ community rehabilitation – specialist multidisciplinary team
Setting	■ home, regional unit, rehabilitation ward
Status of person	■ person will have prognosis of longstanding complex needs requiring specialist medical and multidisciplinary rehabilitation and multi-agency input, such as progressive neurological disease, head injury, complex neurological and physical trauma
Include	■ people requiring specialised multidisciplinary input
Exclude	■ any client whose needs can be met in other programmes stated above

NB: People may move from one category to another

Adapted from Enderby P and Stevenson J (2000). What is intermediate care? Looking at needs. *Managing Community Care* 8(6): 35–40.

Appendix **3** Intermediate care – classification of terms

As part of the work undertaken by the Older Person's Modernisation Team, the South West Regional Office in partnership with the Social Services Inspectorate produced a guide, complementary to the Intermediate Care Circular (HSC 2001/01:LAC (2001)1), to support the next stage development of intermediate care services.

The classification aims to:

- clarify the commonly used terms that form the range of intermediate care services
- identify examples of appropriate situations/patients/conditions for each type of service
- give advice on the available evidence and effectiveness of each service, together with a sample of schemes and contact points that have been developed across the South West Region.

RAPID RESPONSE

Purpose and aims	Examples of appropriate patients/conditions	Effectiveness/evidence and good practice/level of evidence
A service designed to prevent avoidable acute admissions by providing rapid assessment for people referred from GPs, A&E, NHS Direct or social services and (if necessary) immediate access on a 24-hour basis to short-term nursing/therapy support and personal care at home, together with appropriate input from community equipment services and/or housing-based support services	<ul><li>people with a confirmed diagnosis</li><li>minor injuries and infections</li><li>decreased mobility</li><li>falls</li><li>fractures – humerus, wrist, pelvis, ankle, ribs</li><li>mild toxic confusion</li><li>chronic obstructive pulmonary disease</li><li>deep vein thrombosis</li><li>carer breakdown</li></ul>	Rapid response services require a lead time of four to five months when set up to build teams and relationships. These services may take over 12 months to operate at full capacity, with subsequent implications for evaluation

HOSPITAL AT HOME

Purpose and aims	Examples of appropriate patients/conditions	Effectiveness/evidence and good practice/level of evidence
Provides active intensive treatment by health care professionals in the patient's own home for a condition that would otherwise require acute inpatient hospital admission. Can be used either as a way of avoiding an acute admission or to enable earlier discharge from hospital	<ul><li>infections that require intravenous antibiotics (chest, urine, cellulitis)</li><li>people requiring specialist nurse input (continence, stomas, diabetic control)</li><li>people who deteriorate who have a pre-existing muscular/skeletal/neurological disease (e.g. Parkinson's disease)</li><li>early discharge following surgical and orthopaedic procedures</li><li>chemotherapy and blood transfusion</li><li>chronic obstructive pulmonary disease</li><li>fractures – humerus, wrist, ankle, pelvis, ribs</li><li>deep vein thrombosis</li><li>chronic disability exacerbated by acute illness</li></ul>	Evidence that care is as effective as hospital-based care with no clinically important differences in health status, and significantly shorter lengths of stay, in Jeremy Jones, Andrew Wilson, Hilda Parker, Alison Wynn, Carol Jagger, Nicky Spiers and Gillian Parker (1999). Economic evaluation of hospital at home versus hospital care: cost minimisation analysis of data from randomised controlled trial. *British Medical Journal* 319: 1547–50. Review of schemes also suggested positive economic benefits, in Parker G, Bhakta P, Katbamna S, Lovett C, Paisley S, Parker S, Phelps K, Baker R, Jagger C, Lindesay J, Shepperdson B, Wilson A (2000). Best place of care for older people after acute and during sub-acute illness; a systematic review. *Journal of Health Service Research Policy* 5(3) 176–89. <ul><li>North Bristol Trust</li></ul>

RESIDENTIAL/HOSPITAL-BASED REHABILITATION

Purpose and aims	Examples of appropriate patients/conditions	Effectiveness/evidence and good practice/level of evidence
A short-term programme of intensive rehabilitation therapy/care (up to six weeks) in a community hospital or residential setting for people who are medically stable but need a short period of rehabilitation to enable them to re-gain sufficient physical functioning and confidence to return safely to their own home Typically involving input from therapy staff, care managers and nurses, supported by auxiliary care staff, to maximise functional ability and equip person with skills for independent living. May be either step-down, i.e. following stay in acute hospital or step-up, i.e. referral by GP, social services or rapid response team, following full assessment, for people who would otherwise have required admission to an acute hospital, or to longer term residential care	■ may range from around one-to-two weeks (e.g. following pneumonia) to four-to-six weeks (e.g. following major surgery) or slightly longer (e.g. for frail older people recovering from major trauma) ■ people in community hospitals may require medical support from secondary care ■ post general/orthopaedic/ophthalmic surgery ■ trauma ■ cerebrovascular accident ■ mobility problems ■ loss of confidence ■ post pacemaker insertion ■ post infection	Overall evidence shows that residential rehabilitation schemes are successful in terms of outcome, user/carers satisfaction and cost effectiveness, in Audit Commission (2000a). *The way to go home: rehabilitation and remedial services for older people.* London: Audit Commission; Sanderson D and Wright D (1999). *Final evaluation of the CARATS initiatives in Rotherham.* York: York Health Economics Consortium, University of York. Using community hospitals to their full potential can increase acute bed capacity and reduce overall health care costs Some people in community hospitals have a similar level of need to those involved in other models of care which may be more cost effective. There is evidence that people in community hospitals receive lower levels of therapy input than those in residential rehab. units. Herbert G, Townsend J, Ryan J, Wright D, Ferguson B and Wistow G (2000). *Rehabilitation pathways for older people after fractured neck of femur. A study of the impacts of rehabilitation services and social care networks on the aftercare of older people with rehabilitation needs.* Leeds: Nuffield Institute for Health/York Health Economics Consortium. ■ Bath and North East Somerset, Homeward Centre ■ Bournemouth, Broadwaters Unit ■ Cornwall, Homeward Bound ■ Exmouth, Exebank ■ Plymouth, Pierson House (includes four beds for assessment) ■ Weymouth, Buxton House

DOMICILIARY ASSESSMENT AND REHABILITATION

Purpose and aims	Examples of appropriate patients/conditions	Effectiveness/evidence and good practice/level of evidence
Specialist, multidisciplinary team that assesses the needs of people at home or who have just returned home from hospital, and organises packages of services to meet rehabilitation needs. Can facilitate early hospital discharge to continue rehabilitation programme	<ul><li>people with complex needs following transfer of care from hospital</li><li>people who need to learn new techniques/strategies in order to maintain independence</li><li>limb amputation</li><li>Parkinson's disease</li><li>cerebrovascular accident</li><li>falls/risk of falls</li><li>chronic pain (e.g.osteoporosis)</li><li>osteoarthritis</li><li>orthopaedic surgery (e.g. total knee/hip replacement)</li><li>back pain</li><li>frailty</li></ul>	The majority of schemes have physiotherapy and occupational therapy input, but there are significant gaps from other professions (Enderby P and Wade D T (2001). Community rehabilitation in the United Kingdom. *Clinical Rehabilitation* 15(6): 577–81.) The most critical element often missing is effective access to medical assessment and care, in Audit Commission (2000a). *The way to go home: rehabilitation and remedial services for older people.* London: Audit Commission. <ul><li>The Northern Devon Re-ablement Service provides multidisciplinary intermediate care, which encompasses the purpose and aims of several of the schemes as defined in this document.</li><li>Community Rehab Team Network</li><li>Bristol Community Rehab Team</li><li>Mendip PCT</li><li>Ridgeway Downs PCG, Kennet SHARP Scheme (includes residential rehab)</li><li>West Wilts PCT, Swindon Community Rehab Team (includes rapid response, supported discharge)</li></ul>

SUPPORTED DISCHARGE

Purpose and aims	Examples of appropriate patients/conditions	Effectiveness/evidence and good practice/level of evidence
Short-term period of nursing and/or therapeutic support at home with contributory package of home care, sometimes supported by community equipment and/or housing-based support services, enabling people to complete rehab/recovery at home at an earlier stage following an acute hospital stay. Could be provided by community rehabilitation team or dedicated outreach team from local rehabilitation unit. May incorporate home from hospital schemes with support from voluntary organisations	<ul><li>may work well when home has been appropriately designed and equipped for provision of extra support (sheltered housing, etc.)</li><li>post surgical/orthopaedic procedure</li><li>loss of confidence</li><li>falls</li><li>post myocardial infarction</li><li>frailty</li><li>cerebrovascular accident</li><li>depression</li></ul>	May result in substantially lower readmission rates and reduced admission to residential care, in Townsend J, Dyer S, Cooper J, Meade T, Piper M, Frank A (1992). Emergency hospital admissions and readmissions of patients aged over 75 years and the effects of a community-based discharge scheme. In *Health Trends* 24(4): 136–39. Evidence on early discharge schemes appears to suggest significant benefits in enabling people to remain in their own homes, and possibly cost savings for the NHS in Department of Health (2001b). *NSF for Older People.* London: Department of Health Also see Martin F, Oyewole A and Moloney A (1994). A randomized controlled trial of a high support hospital discharge team for elderly people. In *Age and Ageing*, 23(3): 228-34. <ul><li>Cornwall, Home from Hospital, British Red Cross</li><li>Somerset Augmented Care Service providing social care support and uncomplicated nursing care for up to 4 weeks (non-means tested)</li><li>Taunton and Somerset Hospital, Home from Hospital Service, British Red Cross</li></ul>

Day rehabilitation

Purpose and aims	Examples of appropriate patients/conditions	Effectiveness/evidence and good practice/level of evidence
A short-term programme of intensive therapeutic support for up to six weeks, provided at a local authority or private residential home, day hospital or day centre, for people who would otherwise require an inpatient stay. Day hospitals can also provide a one-stop rapid response service with specialist and multidisciplinary input	■ may be used in conjunction with other forms of intermediate care ■ cerebrovascular accident ■ Parkinson's disease ■ limb amputation ■ falls ■ general mobility problems	Evaluation is difficult because of local variation in service provision. Some day hospitals may not be used well because of poor co-ordination, inadequate transport arrangements and poor overall use of time. Access varies by locality. Audit Commission (2000a). *The way to go home: rehabilitation and remedial services for older people*. London: Audit Commission. There remains a need for rigorous systematic evaluation. 'Providers should look at new uses for the day hospital in providing comprehensive elderly care services', from Black D (1998). Remains of the day. *Health Service Journal* 108, issue 5592: 32. ■ Bath, Clara Cross Rehab. Centre ■ Dorchester, Casterbridge Unit, Dorset County Hospital ■ Gloucester Royal Day Hospital (including falls clinic) ■ Salisbury District Hospital, Nunton Day Hospital (including falls clinic) ■ Wincanton, Blackmoor Day Hospital, Verrington Hospital, – health and social care places.

Adapted from NHS Executive South West/SSI South West Regional Office (2001b). *Intermediate care: classification of terms*. Bristol: NHS Executive South West/SSI SWRO. Also available at: www.doh.gov.uk/swro/intermediatecare.pdf

PLANNING THE SERVICE

Commissioners and providers of care services should:
- recognise 'whole-system' dynamics in introducing new services
- ensure membership includes key stakeholders, i.e. acute trust, primary care trust (PCT), social services, housing, clinicians and professionals, independent sector, voluntary agencies and other representatives of relevant existing services
- map existing services available by service provided and geographical area, considering especially the current use of community hospital beds and day hospital/day-care facilities
- make effective use of data on admissions, attempting to quantify admissions that could be responded to if a more appropriate service were in place
- carry out an analysis of referrals based on:
  - top five conditions – consider specialist team (including mental health services)
  - GP referral patterns by practice – identifying outliers
  - periods of peak activity – days of week/hours of day
  - nursing home (NH) support, e.g. analyse number of referrals from NH's or reason for admission from NH's
- agree the remit of the service, including eligibility criteria, sample conditions, follow-up arrangements, appropriate models of delivery and management of referrals that do not meet criteria.

THE SERVICE

With user and carer involvement, the service should aim to provide:
- support to individuals through a crisis – a time-limited service
- supportive discharge from Accident and Emergency wards
- rapid assessment of immediate needs ensuring appropriate medical input/leadership
- prevention of admission to acute hospital by providing appropriate alternatives, including rapid access to diagnostics
- supporting earlier discharge from acute hospital
- a flexible and responsive service with appropriate 24/7 provision and availability
- ability to refer on for further support/treatment/specialist care if required
- links between other local intermediate care services
- agreed follow-through care with community-based services
- an evaluation of the scheme against agreed goals or targets
- explicit and agreed response times. (How rapid is rapid? – same day, within four hours, two hours, 20 minutes?)

ACCESS AND COMMUNICATIONS

- A single point of access is required that is linked to hospital admission systems, local support services, intermediate care providers, SSD, information and advice, e.g. NHS Direct and Care Direct where available.
- Out of hours access should be staffed on a 24/7 basis, supported by appropriate communication systems.
- There should be access to services, such as community equipment services, twilight nursing, interim care.
- There must be clear criteria for access to services with good description and understanding of services available.
- Potential referrers are often unclear about the titles and purpose of schemes. Regular publicity is necessary to increase awareness and take up; this applies equally to primary and secondary care.
- Mechanisms such as patient-held records and a single assessment process should be used to ensure efficient transfer of information.

COMMUNITY TEAM – HEALTH LEAD

Service description and objectives
A multi-disciplinary team, with appropriate medial input and providing a rapid response, typically within 2 hours. Best schemes include rapid access to diagnostics. Interventions limited to 3–7 days with agreed follow up arrangements. Services operate 7 days with extended hours.
May offer a specialist service eg COPD; DVT; TIA; MH; NH support. Includes, or links with, social care services providing a place of safety, twilight nursing or interim care in NH.

Composition: therapists, nurse, SW, doctor, rehab assistants, with admin support

COMMUNITY TEAM – SOCIAL CARE LEAD

Service description
Short-term domiciliary-based service offering intensive social care support. Best schemes include carer support, sitting service, rapid access to housing services (e.g. care and repair) or personal care. Rapid response, typically within 2–4 hours. Interventions limited to 3–7 days with agreed follow-up arrangements. Services operate on 7-day basis with links to out-of-hours services and over-night support.

Composition: Dedicated home carers or rehab assistants (generic or specialist, e.g. MH trained). Service provider may be social services, independent sector and/or voluntary agencies.

HOSPITAL BASED TEAM

Service description and objectives
There are two hospital-based models:
1. Multi-disciplinary team based in A&E/MAU with explicit links with the take team. The team would focus on assessment for alternative to admission and/or initiate discharge planning.
2. Day hospital/rapid-access clinic

Both models include rapid access to diagnostics and specialist opinion. Includes – or links with – social care services providing a place of safety, community rehab teams, twilight nursing or interim care in NH.

Composition: OT, SW, doctor, MH services, PT, rehab assistants

RESIDENTIAL BASED TEAM

Service Description
Includes access to RH/NH. Service may offer both step up and step down beds to avoid admission and support discharge. Best schemes offer observation and assessment, with primary care support and access to medical supervision.
Interventions limited to 3–7 days with agreed follow-up arrangements. Access is available 7 days and over extended hours.

Composition: therapists, nurse, SW, doctor, rehab assistants, care home staff

NB: Examples of each of these models can be found in the SWRO Intermediate Care Compendium, available at www.doh.gov.uk/swro/olderpeopleservices. Adapted from: Plaister I and SWRO (2002) *Managing Inappropriate Admissions: A review of alternatives to admission and characteristics of best practice.* Bristol: SSI/NHS SWRO

AREA/CHECKLIST	EXPECTED OUTCOME	REFERENCE AND FURTHER INFORMATION
Leadership ■ Does a strategic policy making body exist for the partnership? ■ Where appropriate, is there a separate body to oversee implementation of the partnership arrangements? ■ Are the right partners involved – for example should housing, education or leisure services be included?	Strategic partnership body. This will depend on the size and complexity of the partnership arrangements	

Planning
 	
■ Does the proposed partnership arrangement link with local strategic partnerships?
■ Do the arrangements fulfil the objectives identified in the Health Improvement Programme and Community Plan?
■ Do the arrangements meet the targets and milestones outlined for the service. For example in:
  – the National Service Frameworks for mental health and older people?
  – the Valuing People strategy for learning disability services?
  – the circulars on intermediate care and community equipment services?
		Intermediate Care HSC 2001/01: LAC (2001) 1 DoH 2001a
		
		Community Equipment Services HSC2001/008: LAC (2001) 13 DoH 2001d
		Both available at:
		www.doh.gov.uk/coinh.htm

Aims and objectives ■ Is there a clear, measurable plan for delivering the partnership plan? ■ Does it include details of how using the flexibilities will improve services and which groups are likely to benefit? ■ Have all partners agreed the plan? ■ Has the level of co-terminosity between health and local authority populations been agreed? ■ Is the partnership clear who is responsible for delivering the plan?	A joint written agreement including strategy, objectives and planned outcomes. This information forms part of the notification process This forms part of the regulatory framework.	Department of Health guidance on Section 31 Health Act 1999. Available at: DoH 2000c www.doh.gov.uk/jointunit/guidance.htm
Engaging with partners and stakeholders ■ What will the impact of this partnership be on other client groups and services – are there any groups that might lose out? ■ What stakeholders need to be consulted about this partnership? Possibilities include users and carers, independent sector, voluntary groups, trade unions, staff and professional groups. ■ How will the partnership meet the needs of under-represented or disadvantaged groups – for example, minority ethnic communities? ■ Will there be resistance to this partnership. If so, what action will be taken to resolve issues?	Consultation with relevant groups and individuals. This might form part of partners existing approach to consultation and involvement. This forms part of the regulatory framework.	Guidance on consultation available from the Cabinet Office website at: www.cabinet-office.gov.uk/servicefirst/index/consultation.htm

AREA/CHECKLIST	EXPECTED OUTCOME	REFERENCE AND FURTHER INFORMATION
Governance and accountability ■ What form of governance best meets the needs of the partnership? ■ Is there an existing partnership board that this could be part of? ■ How will users and other stakeholders be represented on the partnership? ■ How will the partnership account to the local authority and the NHS for its activity? ■ How will openness and transparency in governance be achieved? ■ Does the performance management process include clear milestones, outcomes and delivery dates? ■ When and how will reviews be carried out on partnership activities ■ Is the partnership clear what it will do if poor performance is reported? ■ What process will be set up to resolve disputes and complaints? ■ Will the proposal meet best value and clinical governance requirements? ■ Are partners clear on the length of the agreement and exit strategy for the partnership?	Forms part of the written agreement and operational protocols. Outcomes might include a partnership board or forum but decisions will depend on: ■ size of the partnership and range of partners ■ complexity of the resource invested ■ whether an existing partnership board exists ■ which stakeholders need to be involved and how best to include them	DH guidance on Section 31 Health Act 1999, available at: as above www.doh.gov.uk/jointunit/ guidance.htm CIPFA guide *Pooled budgets: A Practical Guide for Local and Health Authorities*. Further details can be obtained from: www.cipfa.org.uk/shop Chartered Institute of Public Finance and Accountancy London 2001
Information sharing ■ What information will need to be shared between partners to meet the objectives of the partnership? ■ Are technologies in place to support this? ■ Do these information flows meet the regulations on data protection and confidentiality and also reflect the principles of Caldicott for local councils with social service responsibilities and the NHS? ■ Is there an existing local information sharing group that can co-ordinate protocols and ensure they are appropriate? If not, should there be one?	An agreed information-sharing protocol	DH guidance on Section 31 Health Act 1999. Details can be found at: as above www.doh.gov.uk/jointunit/ info/htm

Managing a pooled budget
 	
■ Are partners agreed on why the flexibility of a pooled fund is required?
■ Have partners agreed to the aims, outcomes and resource to be committed to the fund?
■ Is there a clearly defined criterion for accessing the fund?
■ Are management arrangements for the fund in place?
  – which partner will host the fund?
  – who will be able to access the fund?
  – who will manage it?
  – who will review the pool and how often?
  – what are the auditing arrangements?
  – how long will the pool operate for?
■ Have partners agreed joint eligibility criteria and a single assessment process?
■ Will training be provided for those staff who assess eligibility and access the fund?
■ Are services provided for the fund eligible for charging? If so, is there a process in place to deal with this?
	Pooled health and social care fund for a specific service or client group with clear accountabilities and access arrangements	CIPFA guide *Pooled budgets: a practical guide for local and health authorities*. Further details can be obtained from: www.cipfa.org.uk/shop
		
		As above

AREA/CHECKLIST	EXPECTED OUTCOME	REFERENCE AND FURTHER INFORMATION

Commissioning services
 	
■ Which partner will lead the commissioning process?
■ Have partners agreed the resource to be committed?
■ Have partners agreed the management arrangements for commissioning including:
  – the reporting arrangements?
  – the performance measures to be used?
  – Budget monitoring?
  – Protocols for dealing with delays and slippage in the commissioning process?
  – VAT liabilities for partnership activities?
■ Has the role of the independent sector been taken into account in the commissioning process?
■ Is it clear how contracts will be let by the partnership?
■ Does the lead partner have experience in this area – is training required?
■ Are there charging issues to be resolved and agreed?
	Commissioning agreement	

Integrating provision ■ Have partners agreed an integrated model of care and care pathway(s) for the client group? ■ How will this change be managed – what steps will be taken to support staff? ■ Have partners agreed on the extent for trusted assessments? ■ Have partners agreed clear lines of managerial and professional leadership within the organisation? ■ Have partners agreed how assets will be managed, owned and accounted for. Are there any location issues which hinder partnership working? ■ Have arrangements been put in place to manage the different terms and conditions of staff, including differences in pension arrangements? ■ Will staff be transferred or seconded through this process – has this been negotiated with the relevant bodies? ■ Have you considered what the impact of integrating this service will be on the staff profile of partner organisations? ■ What training will be offered staff and their managers to support and integrate professionals into one structure? ■ Have partners agreed a process for quality assurance (including complaints) which is acceptable both professionally, across agencies and with users and carers?	Integrated single management structure	

AREA/CHECKLIST	EXPECTED OUTCOME	REFERENCE AND FURTHER INFORMATION
Evaluation ■ How will improvements in services be measured? ■ How and when will the outcomes of the partnership be evaluated? ■ What will the partnership do if the outcomes have not been met?	Evaluation process Risk assessment, including an exit strategy	DH guidance available on: www.doh.gov.uk/jointunit/ guidance.htm as above The Nuffield Institute for Health has developed a Partnership Assessment Tool for health and social care. This diagnostic, self-assessment tool is available at: Hardy B, Hudson B and Waddington E (2000) *What makes a good partnership? A partnership assessment tool.* Leeds: Nuffield Institute for Health www.leeds.ac.uk/nuffield/pubs/ index.htm
Notification ■ Once the basis of the partnership arrangement has been established and agreed, the written agreement will need to be defined in writing. This should include details of some of the outcomes listed here. ■ This should be sent together with the Notification Form to the relevant Regional Office	Completed notification form to NHS Regional Office	Notification form is available at: www.doh.gov.uk/jointunit/ appa.htm

Adapted from the Health and Social Care Joint Unit section of the Department of Health website at: www.doh.gov.uk/jointunit/phhaf.htm

Some factors underpinning successful developments to date

In reviewing intermediate care initiatives, attempts have been made to identify factors (Department of Health, 2002a) that seem to be fundamental to successful service commissioning, development and care delivery. When starting the process of moving from visioning to planning and development, it is important to know about, and act on, this information. The following is reproduced in full from the Department of Health paper:

> Local circumstances and models of intermediate care – how they are led professionally and organisationally, how they are structured and delivered – vary enormously. Despite this understandable variability, observation and evidence suggest that, when attempting to explain the apparent success of some services, there are a number of recurrent themes. What underlies good practice and what can others learn from it? Is it just a question of maturity – many examples of good practice have been around a while – or can we 'short circuit' a potentially lengthy process of development?
>
> The list of 'success factors' seems unremarkable in some ways – there is little rocket science and much good sense – but this is a deceptive simplicity. The real achievement of those responsible for planning and delivering successful intermediate care services has been to put into practice apparently simple ideas in a very complex organisational and professional environment. This is no mean feat, which has taken enormous skill and commitment, and which shouldn't be underestimated. Taken together, these factors amount to more than the sum of their individual parts.
>
> This is not an exhaustive list but appears to provide the basis for success, or at least goes some way to explaining it:
>
> ■ **Vision, drive and leadership**. The ability to see beyond existing organisational boundaries and historical patterns of service delivery and to understand the changes that need to be made in order to redesign services more appropriately. Given the range of obstacles facing those breaking new ground and challenging orthodoxies to develop new services, drive and determination are needed in no small measure to make the vision a reality. Added to that, strong leadership to provide the sense of direction and to carry along those who may not yet have glimpsed the vision.
>
> ■ **Senior level commitment** within the organisations involved is essential, to ensure that the appropriate level of resources is committed, that difficult organisational decisions are taken and that those delivering services at the sharp end are empowered to work flexibly in the interests of service users. New ways of working need both permission and protection.
>
> ■ **Shared objectives, clearly articulated and understood**. Clarity of purpose is important for any team, but it is absolutely essential that a team working across organisational and professional boundaries is clear about what it is trying to achieve, is bound together by agreed objectives and is comfortable with the way they are being pursued. These factors are needed both at a strategic/organisational level and at a day-to-day operational level.
>
> ■ **Person-centred care**. Often talked about, but all too often the traditional boundaries, models of care and ways of thinking mitigate against it and there is a tendency to make people fit the available services, rather than the other way around. Simple in theory, maybe less so in practice, but this shift in emphasis can turn many of the usual arguments on their heads. Delivering person-centred care should be a fundamental principle in service design

and delivery, covering the full range of needs, but it can also provide a common focus and 'belief system' for organisations and teams. When achieved, it is a crucial success factor.

- **Strategic and operational management and co-ordination**. There are two roles here and both are needed, though they are unlikely to be embodied within a single person. Effective co-ordination at a 'system' level to make the right organisational connections, maximise impact and service 'coverage' but also at a day-to-day operational level to oil the wheels and ensure that, from a service user's point of view, the service really is seamless. Services certainly need an overall strategy but they also need a 'fixer' able to cut through the organisational complexities. The role of intermediate care co-ordinators as identified in the National Service Framework is vital.

- **Clear appreciation of the potential and limitations** of intermediate care. A willingness to challenge the boundaries of what is possible in delivering safe, appropriate care that promotes independence, but a realisation that such services are not always appropriate. There must be a clear understanding, shared by the organisations, professional groups and individuals involved, of where that boundary lies. Alongside that, there must also be a robust assessment process to identify the individual service users who lie within that boundary, and those who do not.

- **Confidence, trust and accepting risk**. Not built in a day, which is where continuity and service maturity come in, but an essential component of effective partnership working in general, and intermediate care in particular. This again operates at both an organisational level, where there can be many tensions and plenty of historical baggage, and at a professional and personal level, where changing roles and new ideas can present uncomfortable challenges. The single assessment process, and the trust between individuals of different professions that it implies, is a good case in point.

- **Clear professional accountability**. Delivery of intermediate care often involves complex inter-professional and organisational relationships and therefore complex pathways for service users. Despite this complexity, there must be clear accountability for individuals at all times, safeguarding those individuals but also providing a clear framework for those delivering care. It is also important that service users and their carers don't feel lost in a labyrinthine system where they are never sure who is responsible for their care and who to contact.

- **Medical input – clear arrangements**. The intermediate care services reviewed and summarised in this paper are not led by medical staff but all have developed clear local arrangements (though not necessarily formal protocols) to ensure that there is appropriate medical input and access to specialist assessment and diagnosis. There is no doubt that this is one of the key issues and is linked to an understanding of the scope of intermediate care, and its limitations.

- **Shared financial arrangements**. There is plenty of scope for 'border disputes' to get in the way of appropriate, person-centred care. Joint funding of services, with flexibility at the boundaries, is a very positive way of minimising potential disputes and giving practitioners the freedom to meet individuals' needs. These arrangements need not necessarily involve the use of formal pooled budgets or other Health Act flexibilities but they must be clearly set out and agreed by the partners involved, and the rigour required by formal arrangements helps to clarify organisational relationships.

- **Pragmatism, problem solving and open-mindedness**. The task of establishing an effective intermediate care service, either from scratch or by building on existing services, is unlikely to be straightforward. A vision, or an ultimate goal, is important but there will be different ways of getting there. A range of approaches, adaptable to changing circumstances, is a necessary part of the toolkit. Intermediate care, and the environment in which it operates, are not static – as the service grows and evolves there will be a continued need to maintain a pragmatic approach. An open mind is an asset.

■ **Some practicalities – single point of contact, shared base**. Given that fragmentation and lack of co-ordination are important issues in the development of intermediate care, these practical arrangements are also important and shouldn't be underestimated. From a user point of view, whether that's the service user or carer or the person making a referral, a single point of contact for what may be a range of services – ease of access – makes a huge difference, and will affect service take up significantly.

From the service provider's point of view it makes co-ordination much simpler but the co-location of key people from different organisations and professions also gives a greater sense of coherence and of being on the same team.

Reproduced from: Department of Health (2002a). *Intermediate care: moving forward*. London: Department of Health.

1. To be filled in on admission by admitting member of the intermediate care team

- Who made the referral – ie are all potential referrers making use of the scheme?
- Age
- Sex
- Ethnic group
- Postcode (to be mapped to electoral ward)
- GP
- Place of admission for intermediate care eg home, NH (specify), etc.
- Reason for admission (prevent hospital admission or facilitate timely hospital discharge ie shorten the admission)
- Was the patient on the alert register or the case management programme?
- Was intermediate care the first choice for this patient? If not, what was and why was it not used?
- Was this mode of intermediate care the first choice for this patient? If not what was and why was it not used?
- Reason for admission (diagnosis)
- Time from referral to assessment and reasons for delays
- Time from being ready for admission to admission
- Abbreviated mental test score (AMT)
- Barthel index (ADL)
- Waterlow score (pressure sore risk)
- Quality of life measure +/− depression/anxiety score
- If intermediate care was not available, where would the patient have gone, e.g. assessment as O/P, GP, A&E, hospital admission, community district nursing, nursing home, social care package, respite care, hospice?
- For early discharges: How long was the patient in hospital before admission to intermediate care?
- For early discharges: How much longer was the planned hospital stay if no intermediate care team available?
- For admissions from home, what inputs, e.g. home help, district nurse visits, did the patient get before intermediate care admission?
- What was their dependency level?
- What was the proposed discharge date from intermediate care on admission?
- What was the discharge destination envisaged on admission?
- Refusals to go on the scheme

2. To be filled out on discharge or death by a clinical member of the intermediate care team

- Was there a full nursing/'single assessment' assessment? When and by whom?
- Has there been a full medical assessment? When and by whom?
- Is medical cover stated and who is it?
- Was there an identifiable care plan including discharge planning on admission?
- What inputs were provided (therapies, equipment, nursing, medical, carers, informal, voluntary and private) and numbers of visits of each
- Which of the inputs could not have been provided by other existing community services?
- Was there an input that would have particularly helped this patient's recovery but was not available? What was it?
- Abbreviated mental test score (AMT)
- Barthel index (ADL)
- Waterlow score (pressure sore risk)
- Quality of life measure +/− depression/anxiety score
- Untoward events and complications, e.g. confusion, falls, pressure sores, medication errors, violence towards staff
- Was the patient transferred to hospital while under intermediate care, and if so, why?
- Deaths while on scheme and causes
- Discharge destination
- Length of stay on scheme
- What inputs did the patient get on discharge from intermediate care (eg home help, DN visits, etc.)
- Was discharge from intermediate care delayed, for how long and why?
- Requests by patient for transfer to another setting while under intermediate care
- Complaints

---

3. To be given or sent out on discharge

- Patient satisfaction questionnaire
- Carer satisfaction questionnaire
- Referrer satisfaction questionnaire and discharge summary

---

4. To be filled in by an administrative member of the intermediate care team weekly

- Details of any deaths within 28 days of discharge from intermediate care and cause
- Details of any admissions to hospital within 28 days of discharge from intermediate care and reason why
- Complaints
- Number of admissions to each intermediate care team/setting
- Occupancy of each intermediate care team/setting
- Number of bed days used by each intermediate care team/setting
- Number of referred patients not taken on and why, e.g. not suitable (need hospital admission or district nurses could manage), patient refusal or lack of capacity. Team members will need to log all referrals that were not taken on and the reasons.

Adapted from Merton, Sutton and Wandsworth Health Authority (2001). *Intermediate care evaluation framework.* London: MSWHA.

PATIENT/SERVICE USER DETAILS	Service User ID:
Name:	Date of Birth: Sex: Ethnicity code: ☐ M ☐ F ☐
Home Address:	Whereabouts at time of referral: ☐ A&E ☐ sheltered housing ☐ hospital ☐ residential care ☐ own home ☐ IC bed/dom service ☐ nursing home ☐ other (specify) _____
	Postcode: GP code/name:
Diagnosis:	
Date of last clinical assessment: Carried out by: ☐ D/nurse ☐ Physio ☐ OT ☐ CC/ICP	Date of last medical assessment: Carried out by: ☐ Own GP ☐ A&E ☐ Consultant
Reason for referral to IC: ☐ prevent hospital admission ☐ facilitate discharge ☐ prevent admission to long-term care	
If at home: services being received at time of referral: ☐ home care ☐ district nursing ☐ MOW's/frozen meals ☐ community therapy ☐ day care ☐ day hospital	If in hospital: reason for admission: date of admission: predicted LOS:
REFERRAL	Date of referral:
Referred by: ☐ GP ☐ D/N ☐ C/M ☐ A&E ☐ Consultant ☐ other (specify)	
In the opinion of the person making the referral what would have happened to the patient/service user if intermediate care was not available? ☐ sent to A&E ☐ longer stay in hospital ☐ admitted to hospital ☐ admitted to respite care ☐ referred to social services ☐ referred to primary health care team	
IC ASSESSMENT	
Date of assessment:	Assessed by:
Time from referral to assessment: ☐ within 2 hours (urgent) ☐ within 24 hours (non-urgent) ☐ more than 24 hours (delayed) ☐ more than 24 hours (planned)	Assessment outcome: ☐ admitted to IC bed ☐ admitted to domiciliary IC ☐ not admitted for IC
Reason for any delay: ☐ capacity constraint (no IC bed) ☐ capacity constraint (dom-based service) ☐ patient/carer choice ☐ location (out of area) ☐ staffing	Reason for non-admission to IC: ☐ medically unstable ☐ capacity constraint (no IC bed) ☐ capacity constraint (dom-based service) ☐ refusal ☐ does not meet IC criteria
Outcome for those not admitted to IC ☐ sent to A&E ☐ admitted to hospital ☐ referred to social services ☐ referred to mental health services	 ☐ longer stay in hospital ☐ admitted to respite care ☐ referred to primary health care team
Were rehab goals set on admission to IC? ☐ Yes ☐ No	Was discharge plan set on admission to IC? ☐ Yes ☐ No

Date care plan agreed:		Date discharge plan agreed:	
Expected discharge date:		Expected discharge destination:	
Time from assessment to admission:		Reason for any delay:	

Time from assessment to admission:
- ☐ within 2 hours (urgent)
- ☐ within 24 hours (non-urgent)
- ☐ more than 24 hours (delayed)
- ☐ more than 24 hours (planned)

Reason for any delay:
- ☐ medical deterioration
- ☐ no IC bed available
- ☐ domiciliary IC capacity constraint
- ☐ transport constraint
- ☐ patient/carer choice

OUTCOMES

Date of discharge:

Was discharge from IC delayed?
☐ Yes *If yes, number of days...*   ☐ No

Discharge destination:
- ☐ own home
- ☐ hospital
- ☐ residential home
- ☐ nursing home
- ☐ sheltered accommodation
- ☐ other (specify) _____

Reason for delayed discharge from IC:
- ☐ deterioration in patient's condition
- ☐ carer issues
- ☐ housing issues
- ☐ awaiting health care package
- ☐ awaiting social services care package
- ☐ awaiting therapy care package
- ☐ awaiting equipment
- ☐ other (specify) _____

Medical cover for IC provided by: ☐ own GP   ☐ temp GP   ☐ IC specialist GP/consultant

Were any difficulties experienced with medical cover? ☐ Yes   ☐ No

If Yes, please specify:

	ADMISSION	DISCHARGE	CHANGE
Barthel ADL index			
AMT score			
Waterlow Pressure score			
Quality of life measure			

In the view of IC co-ordinator, were goals achieved? ☐ Yes ☐ Partially ☐ No

In the view of patient/service user, were goals achieved? ☐ Yes ☐ Partially ☐ No

What input was provided during IC episode?
- ☐ medical   No of visits
- ☐ nursing   No of visits
- ☐ OT   No of visits
- ☐ physio   No of visits
- ☐ speech and language therapy
- ☐ health care support worker
- ☐ rehab assistant
- ☐ social worker/care manager
- ☐ other (specify) _____

Equipment provided:

What services are being received as part of discharge care plan?
- ☐ crisis care/HDT
- ☐ home care
- ☐ district nursing
- ☐ MOW's/frozen meals
- ☐ community therapy
- ☐ day care
- ☐ day hospital
- ☐ shopping service
- ☐ OPP

Which of these inputs could not have been provided by other exisiting community services and why? (Include reasons relating to frequency/intensity of input.)

Were there any services/inputs that would have assisted earlier discharge had they been available?   ☐ Yes ☐ No
If yes, specify:

If admitted to hospital while receiving IC, reason for admission:

Any other untoward events during IC intervention? ☐ Yes ☐ No (attach details)

If died while on IC cause of death:

Complaints or requests to transfer to another care setting? ☐ Yes ☐ No (attach details)

User Satisfaction Questionnaire Issued?	☐ Yes ☐ No
Carer Satisfaction Questionnaire Issued?	☐ Yes ☐ No

Adapted from Merton and Sutton PCT (2002). *Data collection proforma*. London: MSPCT

Bibliography

The bibliography lists all publications referenced in the text. Other sources are listed in the 'Further reading' list at the end of each section.

Ansoff H I (1965). *Corporate strategy: an analytic approach to business policy for growth and expansion*. New York: McGraw-Hill.

Audit Commission (in press). *Older people and whole systems working* (working title). London: Audit Commission.

Audit Commission (2002). *Fully equipped 2002: assisting independence*. London: Audit Commission.

Audit Commission (2000a). *The way to go home: rehabilitation and remedial services for older people*. London: Audit Commission.

Audit Commission (2000b). *Fully equipped: the provision of equipment to older or disabled people by the NHS and some services in England and Wales*. London: Audit Commission.

Audit Commission (1997). *The coming of age: improving care services for older people*. London: Audit Commission.

Banks P (2002). *Partnerships under pressure. A commentary on progress in partnership working between the NHS and local government*. London: King's Fund.

Banks P (1998). *The carers' compass*. London: King's Fund.

Black D (1998). Remains of the day. *Health Service Journal* 108, issue 5592: 32.

Borrill C, Carletta J, Carter J, Dawson J, Garrod S, Rees A, Richards A, Shapiro D and West M (2001). *The effectiveness of health care teams in the National Health Service*. Aston: Aston Centre for Health Services Research (ACHSOR).

Borrill C and West M (2001a). *Developing team working in health care. A guide for managers*. Aston: ACHSOR.

Borrill C and West M (2001b). *How good is your team? A guide for team members*. Aston: ACHSOR.

Borrill C, West M, Dawson J, Shapiro D, Rees A, Richards A, Garrod S, Carletta J and Carter A (2001c). *Team working and effectiveness in health care. Findings from the health care team effectiveness project*. Aston: ACHSOR.

Bours G J, Ketelaars C A, Frederiks C, Abu-Saad H and Wouters E (1998). The effects of aftercare on chronic patients and frail elderly patients when discharged from hospital: a systematic review. *Journal of Advanced Nursing* 27: 1076–86.

Burch S and Borland C (1999). A randomised controlled trial of day hospital and day centre therapy. *Clinical Rehabilitation* 13: 105–12.

Cameron I, Crotty M, Currie C, Finnegan T, Gillespie L, Gillespie W, Handoll H, Kurrle S, Madhok R, Murray G, Quinn K and Torgerson D (2000). Geriatric rehabilitation following fractures in older people: a systematic review. *Health Technology Assessment* 4: 2.

Campbell H, Karnon J and Dowie R (2001). Cost analysis of a hospital-at-home initiative using discrete event simulation. *Journal of Health Services Research and Policy* 6(1): 14–22.

Carpenter I (1998). Standardised assessment in the community. In Challis D, Darton R, Stewart K, editors. *Community care, secondary health care and care management*. Canterbury: University of Kent PSSRU/Ashgate Publishing.

Challis D, Darton R, Johnson L, Stone M and Traske K (1995). *Care management and health care of older people: the Darlington Community Care Project*. Aldershot: Arena.

Clinical Audit Unit (1999). *Nursing home placements for older people in England and Wales: a national audit 1995–1998*. London: St George's Hospital Medical School Department of Geriatric Medicine.

Coast J, Richards S, Peters T, Gunnell D, Darlow M-A and Pounsford J (1998). Hospital at home or acute hospital care? A cost minimisation analysis. *British Medical Journal* 316(7147): 1802–6.

Cox S, Wilcock P and Young J (1999). Improving the repeat prescribing in a busy general practice. A study using continuous quality improvement methodology. *Quality in Health Care* 1999 8(2): 119–25.

Damiani M and Dixon J (2002). *Managing the pressure: emergency admissions in London 1997 to 2001*. London: King's Fund.

Department of Health (2002a). *Intermediate care: moving forward*. London: Department of Health.

Department of Health (2002b). Joint Investment Plans (JIPs) for Older People/Intermediate Care. *Chief Executive's Bulletin*, March 28. London: Department of Health. Available at: www.doh.gov.uk/cebulletin28march.htm#15

Department of Health (2002c). The single assessment process for older people. HSC 2002/01: LAC 2002(1). London: Department of Health. Available at: www.doh.gov.uk/scg/sap/hsc200201.htm

Department of Health (2002d). *The single assessment process: assessment tools and scales*. London: Department of Health.

Department of Health (2002e). *Care homes for older people. National minimum standards (Care Standards Act 2000)*. London: Department of Health.

Department of Health (2002f). *Delivering the NHS Plan: next steps on investment, next steps on reform*. CM5503. London: The Stationery Office.

Department of Health (2002g). *Performance ratings for social services (England) 2001/02*. London: Social Services Inspectorate.

Department of Health (2001a). *Intermediate care*. HSC 2001/1: LAC (2001) 1. London: Department of Health.

Department of Health (2001b). National Service Framework for Older People. London: Department of Health.

Department of Health (2001c). *Residential care, housing, care and support schemes and 'Supporting People'. A consultation paper*. London: Department of Health.

Department of Health (2001d). *Community equipment services*. HSC 2001/008: LAC (2001)13. London: Department of Health.

Department of Health (2001e). *Guide to integrating community equipment services*. London: Department of Health.

Department of Health (2001f). 'Cash for Change' initiative to tackle 'bedblocking'. Press release 2001/0464, 9 October 2001.

Department of Health (2001g). *Guidance on the grant for building care capacity*. LAC(2001)34. London: Department of Health.

Department of Health (2001h). *Building capacity and partnership in care: an agreement between the statutory and the independent social care, health care and housing sectors*. London: Department of Health.

Department of Health (2001i). *Implementing the NHS Plan: developing services following the National Beds Inquiry*. HSC 2001/03: LAC (2001)4. London: Department of Health.

Department of Health (2000a). *The NHS Plan: a plan for investment, a plan for reform*. London: Department of Health.

Department of Health (2000b). *Shaping the future NHS: long term planning for hospital and related services. Consultation document on the findings of the National Beds Inquiry*. London: Department of Health.

Department of Health (2000c). *Guidance on the Health Act Section 31 partnership arrangements*. London: Department of Health. Available at: www.doh.gov.uk/jointunit/psip1.htm#pooled

Department of Health (1999a). The Health Act 1999. London: The Stationery Office.

Department of Health (1999b). *Promoting independence: partnership, prevention and carers grants – conditions and allocations 1999/2000*. LAC(99)13.

Department of Health (1999c). *Improving quality and performance in the new NHS. Clinical indicators and high level performance indicators*. HSC 1999/139. London: Department of Health.

Department of Health (1999d). *A new approach to social services performance: consultation responses and confirmation of performance indicators*. LAC (99)27. London: Department of Health.

Department of Health (1998a). *Better services for vulnerable people: maintaining the momentum*. Letter from NHS Executive of Chief Executives of Health Authorities and NHS Trusts and Social Services Directors, 20 August.

Department of Health (1998b). *Modernising social services*. London: Department of Health.

Department of Health (1997a). *Better services for vulnerable people: maintaining the momentum*. EL(97)62, CI(97)24. London: Department of Health.

Department of Health (1997b). *The new NHS: modern, dependable*. London: Department of Health.

Department of Health (1990). *National Health Service and Community Care Act*. London: The Stationery Office.

Dunn R B (1996). The role of post-hospital discharge schemes. Current medical literature. *Geriatrics* 27: 1076–86.

Enderby P and Stevenson J (2000). What is intermediate care? Looking at needs. *Managing Community Care* 8(6): 35–40.

Enderby P and Wade D T (2001). Community rehabilitation in the United Kingdom. *Clinical Rehabilitation* 15(6): 577–81.

Fear J (2000). 'Reconfiguring older people's services in Leeds'. Presentation to King's Fund conference 'Developing rehabilitation opportunities for older people: a strategic approach', 12 May 2000. Manchester: Manchester University.

Fletcher P, Riseborough M, Humphries J, Jenkins C and Whittingham P (1999). Citizenship and services in older age: the strategic role of very sheltered housing. In *Housing* 21.

Foote C and Stanners C (2002). *Integrating services for older people*. London: Jessica Kingsley Publishers.

Forster A, Young J and Langhorne P (1999). Systematic review of day hospital care for elderly people. *British Medical Journal* (7187) 318: 837–41.

Forte P, Bowen T, Foote C and Poxton R (2002). *Intermediate care: getting the balance right*. London: Balance of Care Group.

Gladman J, Lincoln N, Adams S (1993). Use of the extended ADL scale with stroke patients. *Age and Ageing* 22: 419–24.

Goddard M, McDonagh M and Smith D (2000). Avoidable use of beds and cost-effectiveness of care in alternative locations (Annex E). In *Shaping the future NHS: long term planning for hospitals and related services. Consultation document on the findings of the National Beds Inquiry: supporting analysis*. London: Department of Health.

Goddard M, McDonagh M and Smith D (1999). *Acute hospital care: Final report*. York: Centre for Health Economics.

Godfrey M (1999). *Preventative strategies for older people – mapping the literature on effectiveness and outcomes*. Oxford: Anchor Trust.

Godfrey M, Randall T, Long A and Grant M (2001). *Review of effectiveness and outcomes: home care*. Exeter: Centre for Evidence Based Social Services. Available at: www.ex.ac.uk/cebss/files/HomeCare.pdf

Griffiths P, Wilson-Barnett J, Richardson G, Spilsbury K, Miller F, Harris R (2000). The effectiveness of intermediate care in a nursing-led inpatient unit. *International Journal of Nursing Studies* 37(2): 153–61.

Hanford L, Easterbrook L and Stevenson J (1999). *Rehabilitation for older people: the emerging policy agenda*. London: King's Fund.

Help the Aged Health of Older People Group (2000). *Our future health*. London: Help the Aged.

Herbert G (2002). *Tomlinson Court: a new approach to rehabilitation in sheltered housing. Evaluation report*. Leeds: Nuffield Institute for Health.

Herbert G, Townsend J, Ryan J, Wright D, Ferguson B and Wistow G (2000). *Rehabilitation pathways for older people after fractured neck of femur. A study of the impacts of rehabilitation services and social care networks on the aftercare of older people with rehabilitation needs*. Leeds: Nuffield Institute for Health/York Health Economics Consortium.

Huusko T, Karppi P, Avikainen V, Kautiainen H and Sulkava R (2000). Randomised, clinically controlled trial of intensive geriatric rehabilitation in patients with hip fracture: subgroup analysis of patients with dementia. *British Medical Journal* (7269) 321: 1107–11.

Hyde C J, Robert I E and Sinclair A J (2000). The effects of supporting discharge from hospital to home in older people. *Age and Ageing* 29(3): 271–79.

Ibbotson M (2001). 'Community Health Sheffield (NHS) Trust Community Rehabilitation Unit, working in partnership'. Presentation to King's Fund workshop 'Nursing homes and intermediate care', 20 March 2001. Manchester: Manchester University.

Iles V and Sutherland K (2001). *Organisational change*. London: NCC SDO R&D. Available at: www.sdo.lshtm.ac.uk/PDF/ChangeManagementReview.pdf

Independent Healthcare Association (2002). *Engaging the independent sector in the development of intermediate care*. London: Independent Healthcare Association.

Kalra L, Evans A, Perez I, Knapp M, Donaldson N and Swift C (2000). Alternative strategies for stroke care: a prospective randomised controlled trial. *The Lancet* (9233) 356: 894–9.

Kaplan R S and Norton D P (1992). The balanced scorecard: measures that drive performance. *The Harvard Business Review* Jan–Feb 1992: 71–9.

Kent J, Payne C, Stewart M and Unell J (2002). *External evaluation of the Home Care Reablement Pilot Project.* Leicester: De Montfort University Centre for Group Care and Community Studies.

King's Fund (2001a). *Preventing dependency and promoting independence of older people: key issues for improving performance in health and social care.* London: King's Fund.

King's Fund (2001b). Rehabilitation Development Network. *News Update 7.* London: King's Fund.

Le Mesurier N (2001a). *Evaluation of five social rehabilitation projects supported by Age Concern England: aims, working methods and alliances.* First interim report. Birmingham: Social Science in Medicine Group, University of Birmingham.

Le Mesurier N (2001b). *Evaluation of five social rehabilitation projects supported by Age Concern England.* Second interim report: Case studies and performance data. Birmingham: Social Science in Medicine Group, University of Birmingham.

Lewin K (1951). *Field theory in social science.* New York: Harper Row.

Lymbery M (2002). Transitional residential rehabilitation: what helps to make it work? *MCC: Building knowledge for integrated care* 10(1): 43–8.

Merton, Sutton and Wandsworth Health Authority (2001). *Intermediate care evaluation framework.* London: MSWHA.

Merton and Sutton PCT (2002). *Data collection proforma.* London: MSPCT.

Middleton S and Roberts A (2000). *Integrated care pathways: a practical approach to implementation.* Oxford: Butterworth-Heinemann.

National Co-ordinating Centre for NHS Service Delivery and Organisation (2001). *Making informed decisions on change.* London: NCC SDO R&D.

NHS Centre for Reviews and Dissemination (1999). Getting evidence into practice. *Effective Health Care* 5: 1.

NHS Executive (2000). *Workforce and development: getting people on board*, July: 4.

NHS Executive South West/SSI South West Regional Office (2001a). *Intermediate care: initial diagnostic tool.* Bristol: NHS Executive South West/SSI SWRO.

NHS Executive South West/SSI South West Regional Office (2001b). *Intermediate care: classification of terms.* Bristol: NHS Executive South West/SSI SWRO.

Nocon A and Baldwin S (1998). *Trends in rehabilitation policy: a review of the literature.* London: King's Fund/Audit Commission.

Nolan M and Caldock K (1996). Assessment: identifying the barriers to good practice. *Health and Social Care in the Community* 4(2): 77–85.

Northumberland Health Action Zone Person Centred Care Programme (2000). *Show me the way to go home! Developing rehabilitation opportunities for older people in Northumberland. Whole systems event report.* Morpeth: Northumberland HAZ.

Nuffield Institute for Health (2001). Accompanying papers, Policy into Practice Seminar Series: Intermediate care: rehabilitation, recuperation or warehousing. West Yorkshire Playhouse, 22 February.

Olve N-G, Roy J and Wetter M (1999). *Performance drivers: a practical guide to using the balanced scorecard.* London: John Wiley.

Parker G (2002). 'What works and what doesn't in intermediate care?' Presentation to King's Fund/BMA Age Concern England conference on intermediate care, 18 March 2002. London: BMA House.

Parker G, Bhakta P, Katbamna S, Lovett C, Paisley S, Parker S, Phelps K, Baker R, Jagger C, Lindesay J, Shepperdson B, Wilson A (2000). Best place of care for older people after acute and during sub-acute illness; a systematic review. *Journal of health service research policy* 5(3) 176–89.

Penrice G M, Simpson L, de Caestecker L, Brown G and Gillies S (2001). Low dependency residents in private nursing homes in Glasgow. *Health Bulletin* 59(1): 4–9.

Philp, Prof. I (2000). 'Intermediate care: the evidence base in practice'. Presentation at the Royal College of Physicians/British Geriatric Society, 30 November. London: RCP.

Plaister I. *Managing inappropriate admissions: a review of alternatives to admission and characteristics of best practice*. Bristol: SSI South West Regional Office/NHSE, 2002.

Robinson J and Batstone G (1996). *Rehabilitation: a development challenge*. London: King's Fund.

Robinson J and Turnock S (1998). *Investing in rehabilitation*. London: King's Fund.

Rollins H (2002). Stopping the malnutrition carousel. *Community Practitioner* 75(1): 12–13.

Royal College of Physicians (2002). *Nutrition and patients: a doctor's responsibility*. London: RCP.

Sander R (2000). *Evaluation of the Portsmouth and South East Hampshire Community Rehabilitation Project*. Portsmouth: University of Portsmouth School of Health and Social Care.

Sanderson D and Wright D (1999). *Final evaluation of the CARATS initiatives in Rotherham*. York: York Health Economics Consortium, University of York.

Senge P (1990). *The fifth discipline: the art and practice of the learning organisation*. London: Doubleday/Century Business.

Shepperd S and Iliffe S (2002). Hospital at home versus in-patient hospital care (Cochrane Review), *The Cochrane Library* 2. Available at: www.update-software.com/abstracts/ ab000356.htm

Sinclair A and Dickinson E (1998). *Effective practice in rehabilitation: the evidence of systematic reviews*. London: King's Fund/Audit Commission.

Spencer L (2000). *Rehabilitation and rapid response services*. Briefing Paper 6. London: King's Fund.

Steiner A, Walsh B, Pickering R, Wiles R, Ward J and Brooking J (2001a). Therapeutic nursing or unblocking beds? A randomised controlled trial of a post-acute intermediate care unit. *British Medical Journal* (7284) 322: 453–60.

Steiner A (2001b). Intermediate care: more than 'a nursing thing'. *Age and Ageing* 30: 433–35.

Steiner A (2001c). Intermediate care: a good thing? *Age and Ageing* 30: 30–39.

Steiner A (2000). 'Evidence and evaluation'. Presentation to King's Fund conference 'Care closer to home', 15 September. London, Ambassadors Hotel.

Steiner A (1997). *Intermediate care: a conceptual framework and review of the literature*. London: King's Fund.

Steiner A, Vaughan B and Hanford L (1998). *Intermediate care: approaches to evaluation*. London: King's Fund.

Stevenson J (2001a). Singing from the same hymn sheet. *Community Care* 29 March, 22–3.

Stevenson J (2001b). *Mapping local rehabilitation and intermediate care services*. London: King's Fund.

Stevenson J (2001c). *NHS responsibilities for meeting continuing health care needs for people who live in nursing homes or residential care homes*. London: King's Fund.

Stevenson J (2000). Rehabilitation services. In: Merry P, editor. *Wellard's NHS Handbook 2000–01*. Wadhurst: JMH Publishing.

Stevenson J (1999). *Comprehensive assessment of older people*. Briefing Paper 2. London: King's Fund.

Stroke Unit Trialists' Collaboration, Langhorne P *et al*. (1997). Collaborative systematic review of the randomised trials of organised inpatient (stroke unit) care after stroke. *British Medical Journal* 314: 1151–9.

Stuck A, Siu A, Wieland G, Adams J and Rubenstein L (1993), Comprehensive geriatric assessment: a meta analysis of controlled trials. *The Lancet* 342: 1032–36.

NHS Executive South West/Social Services Inspectorate South West Regional Office (2002). *Modernising services for older people: a compendium of intermediate care and other recent initiatives in place or under development in the south west*. Issue 4, February 2002. Available at www.doh.gov.uk/swro/intermediatecare.pdf

Trappes-Lomax T, Ellis A, Fox M, Taylor R, Stead J, Power M and Bainbridge I (2002a). *Buying time: an evaluation of the effectiveness and cost-effectiveness of a joint health/social care residential rehabilitation unit for older people on discharge from hospital*. Exeter: University of Exeter.

Trappes-Lomax T, Ellis A, Fox M, Rohini T, Stead J and Sweeney K (2002b). *The user voice: a qualitative study of user views about 'what worked and what could have worked better' at a joint health/social care short-term residential rehabilitation unit for older people*. Exeter: University of Exeter.

Vaughan B and Lathlean J (1999). *Intermediate care: models in practice*. London: King's Fund.

Vaughan B and Withers G (2002). Acute distress. *Health Service Journal* 5804 9 May: 24–7.

Walker M F, Gladman J, Lincoln N, Siemonsma P and Whiteley T (1999). Occupational therapy for stroke patients not admitted to hospital: a randomised controlled trial. *The Lancet* Issue 9175; 354: 278–80.

Ward D, Severs M and Dean T (2001). *Care home environments: rehabilitation and older persons. A report of stage one of a national survey*. Portsmouth: University of Portsmouth School of Postgraduate Medicine.

Wiles R, Postle K, Steiner A and Walsh B (in press). Nurse-led intermediate care: patients' perceptions. *International Journal of Nursing Studies*

Wilson A, Wynn A and Parker H (2002). Patient and carer satisfaction with 'hospital at home': quantitative and qualitative results from a randomised controlled trial. *British Journal of General Practice* 52(474): 9–13.

Wilson K and Stevenson J (2001). *Intermediate care co-ordination: the function*. London: King's Fund.

Wistow G, Waddington E and Fong Chiu L (2002). *Intermediate care: balancing the system*. Leeds: Nuffield Institute for Health

Young J and Forster A (1992). The Bradford community stroke trial: results at six months. *British Medical Journal* 304: 108–9.

Younger-Ross S and Lomax T (1998). Outlands: five years on. *Managing Community Care* 1998; 6(1): 37–40.

Index

Page numbers in *italics* refer to tables, *a* indicates appendices.

access 49, 87
  to medical cover 76–7
accident and emergency (A&E)
  departments 27
action plan 64, *65*
acute hospitals 23–4, *47*
appropriateness evaluation protocol
  (AEP) 50
assessment 34, 78, 81–4
  intermediate care and specialist
    medical 76–7
  see also evaluation; needs
Audit Commission 12, 13, 21–2, 33, 46,
  67–8

balance of care approach 60–1
'balanced scorecard' evaluation method
  92–3
benchmarks for assessment practice 84
bottlenecks in service provision 49

care at home *see* home care
care closer to home 11
care outcomes, tools/measures *94*
care packages *47*
carers
  consulting 78
  increase in age of 46
  perceptions of Hospital at Home
    (HaH) 26
  perceptions of nurse-led units 28
  rehabilitation role 76
case studies 53–6
change
  commissioning/contracting for 42
  cycle of 21–2
  demographic 46
  management 68–74
  operational implications of 74–7
  readiness and capability 72–3
  redesigning existing systems 77–8
  securing individual behaviour 74
clients *see* user(s)
co-ordinator roles 84–5, 88–9, *117a*,
  118a
Commission for Health Improvement 12
commissioning/contracting
  appropriate services 87–8
  for change 42
  independent sector 79–80
  responsibilities of co-ordinators 88
  shared values and principles 43,
    44, 52
commitment 67, 72, *73*, *116a*

community care
  assessment tools *83*
  see also home care; *specific services*
community hospitals 27, 36, *47*
community rehabilitation
  cost effectiveness 27
  funding 14
compliance 72, *73*
consulting
  with clients and carers 78
  with stakeholders 53, 57, 64
continuity of care 78
contracting *see* commissioning/
  contracting
cost effectiveness
  community rehabilitation 27
  Hospital at Home (HaH) 26
  Rapid Response 27
  residential rehabilitation units 28
  tools/measures *94*
costs
  fractured neck of femur 32
  research projects 35, 36
  see also funding
cross-agency working *see* partnership
  arrangements; team working;
  'whole systems' approach
cycle of change 21–2

day care centres 30–1
day hospitals 30–1
day rehabilitation 30–1, *109a*
day services 30–1, *47*
dementia 33
  extra-care supported housing 30
demographic change 46
Department of Health
  assessment guidelines 81, 82–3
  co-ordination of care 84–5
  commissioning guidelines 79–80
  definition of intermediate care 5–7, 8
  -funded research 35–6
  funding 15
  initiatives for intermediate care 10–14
  intermediate care and medical cover
    76–7
  mental health services 33
  partnership arrangements 45, 62–3
  success factors 67–8, 116–18a
depression 33
diagnostic tool *see* Initial Diagnostic
  Tool
domiciliary care *see* home care
drive for change 67, *116a*

drivers of intermediate care 13–14
early/supported discharge schemes 26,
  108a
eligibility criteria 49
enabling model
  rehabilitation assistant, role 76
  vs caring model of nursing 28, 29–30
  see also independence
enrolment 72, *73*
equipment services 33–4
equity 49
evaluation 87, 88
  continuous *95*
  data collection proforma 121–2a
  framework/model 92–3, 119–20a
  importance of 91
  tools/measures 50, *93*, *94*, 99–102a
  see also assessment; needs
evidence *see* research
extra-care supported housing 30

force field analysis 71–2
fractured neck of femur 32
funding 14–16, 86
  increases 45, 46
  joint 63, *117a*
  pooling of budgets 59, 62–3
  see also cost effectiveness; costs

gaps in service provision 48–9

HaH *see* Hospital at Home
Health Act (1999) 14, 62–3
  checklist 112–15a
health care teams 74–5
Health Improvement Programmes
  (HImPs) 14
hip fracture 32
home care 31, 45, *47*, *108a*
  Hospital at Home (HaH) 25–6, *106a*
  rehabilitation assistant, role 76
  stroke 32–3
hospital admission
  alternatives to 25–7
  avoidance strategies 24–5, 45, 50, 77,
    110, *111a*
  'vicious circle' of 21
Hospital at Home (HaH) 25–6, *106a*
hospital discharge schemes,
  early/supported 26, *108a*
hospital(s)
  acute 23–4, *47*
  day 30–1
  rehabilitation in 20, 22, *107a*

housing issues 46

independence 7, 10, 45
  see also enabling model
independent sector
  commissioning/contracting 79–80
  see also nursing homes
information, about service models 62
information sharing 82, 84, 87
information technology 82
Initial Diagnostic Tool 50, 99–102a
integrated care *vs* patient pathways
  77–8
intermediate care
  classification of terms 106–9a
  definitions 5–9
  drivers of 13–14
  vs other forms of care 6–7
  vs rehabilitation 8
intermediate care co-ordinator, roles
  84–5, 88–9, 117a, 118a

joint funding 63, 117a
Joint Investment Plans (JIPs) 14, 86
joint working arrangements *see*
  partnership arrangements; team
  working; 'whole systems' approach

leadership 67, 68, 116a
league tables, social services 15–16
local circumstances
  case studies 53–6
  charging policies 49
  national policy and 45–6
local implementation of NSF 84–5, 86
local services, publicising 81

malnutrition 31
medical assessment/cover 76–7
mental health *see* dementia;
  depression
Mid-Hants Primary Care Trust (case
  study) 54–6

National Beds Inquiry, The 11, 13
National Co-ordination Centre for NHS
  Service Delivery and Organisation
  68–9
National Insurance (NI) 15
National Service Framework (NSF) for
  Older People 12–13, 14, 19
local implementation 84–5, 86
needs
  consulting with stakeholders 53, 57,
    64
  matching services to 51–2
  see also assessment; evaluation
NHS and Community Care Act (1990) 21
NHS Plan 11–12, 14, 26, 74
  Option Three: Care closer to home 11
Northumberland Health Action Zone
  (case study) 53–4
Nuffield Institute for Health (case study)
  55–6

nurse-led units (NLUs) 28
nursing homes 24, 29–30, 47

occupational therapy 33, 75
operational aspects 74–7, 87–8
  research 34–5

partnership arrangements 12, 31, 45,
  62–3
  see also team working; 'whole
    systems' approach
patients *see* user(s)
person-centred care 13, 33, 45, 82,
  116–17a
physiotherapy 33, 75, 76
point prevalence studies 50–1
  evidence from 23–4
pooling of budgets 59, 62–3
preventative services 13, 23, 45
primary care 25, 27
  groups/trusts 13–14, 82
processes evaluation, tools/measures
  94
publicising local services 81

randomised controlled trials (RCTs) 19
Rapid Response 26–7, 106a
readiness to change 72–3
referrals 49
rehabilitation 12, 13–14, 47, 53
  community 27
  day 30–1, 109a
  functions of (Sheffield definition)
    103–5a
  limitations of research 19–20
  residential units 28–9
  shortcomings of current
    arrangements 20–3
  social 34, 80
  vs intermediate care 8
rehabilitation assistant, role 76
rehabilitation teams 75–6
research
  current government-funded 35–6
  operational aspects 34–5
  types and their limitations 19–20
  see also case studies; point
    prevalence studies
residential care 24, 27–30, 47
  assessment tools 83
residential rehabilitation 107a
  units 28–9

services
  delivery, co-ordinator roles 88–9
  equipment 33–4
  evaluation *see* evaluation
  hypothetical system 48
  information about individual models
    62
  layers of provision 57
  mapping existing 46–51
  matching to needs 51–2
  preventative 13, 23, 45

publicising 81
  types and effectiveness of 25–31
  voluntary sector 34, 80
shared information 82, 84, 87
shared objectives 116a
shared values and principles 43, 44, 52
sheltered housing 30, 47
social care
  balance of care approach 61
  residential rehabilitation units 28, 29
social inclusion 46
social rehabilitation 34, 80
social services
  league tables 15–16
  partnership arrangements 12, 31, 45,
    62–3
Social Services Inspectorate 12
Social Services Performance
  Assessment Framework 26
specialist medical assessment/cover
  76–7
stakeholders 45, 50–1
  consulting 53, 57, 64
strategic development 86–9
stroke 32–3
stroke units 32
success factors 67–8, 116–18a
supported/early discharge schemes 26,
  108a
SWOT analysis 69–70

team leadership 68
team working 35, 45, 74–6, 111a
  assessments 82
  balance of care model 60
  co-ordinator roles 84–5, 88–9, 117a,
    118a
  information sharing 82, 84, 87
  integrated care *vs* patient pathways
    77–8
  stroke units 32
  see also partnership arrangements;
    'whole systems' approach

user(s)
  consulting with 78
  patient pathways 77–8
  satisfaction
    Hospital at Home (HaH) 26
  tools/measures 94

values and principles, shared 43, 44, 52
'vicious circle', of hospital admission 21
vision 67, 116a
voluntary sector 34, 80

'whole systems' approach 21–2, 45–6,
  47, 48, 53
  effectiveness of 56–7
  limitations of research in identifying
    19, 20
  success factors 67–8, 116–18a
  see also partnership arrangements;
    team working

Acknowledgements

We would like to thank all the people who have worked with the King's Fund Programme 'Developing Rehabilitation Opportunities for Older People'. In particular, thanks are due to members of the Rehabilitation Development Network supported by the programme, who freely shared information and ideas. They taught us a lot about the development of innovative rehabilitative care, and made it possible for us to put together this guide on ways to take forward the intermediate care development agenda.

We are also grateful to those people and organisations who have granted permission for us to use material in this guide and to the Department of Health, which provided a grant towards the production costs.

Related King's Fund titles

Intermediate Care
MODELS IN PRACTICE
Barbara Vaughan and Judith Lathlean

Should intermediate care services replace other services, and how should they be developed? This publication explores these questions and describes current services from different parts of the UK. It describes how services vary in different settings and in different organisations.

ISBN 1 85717 273 6   May 1999   114pp   Price £10.99

Intermediate Care
A DISCUSSION PAPER
Andrea Steiner and Barbara Vaughan

Where is the proper locus of intermediate care, and who should lead care provision? These were some of the issues debated at the King's Fund seminar held in October 1996. This report provides a detailed summary of the outcomes of the seminar and includes a list of the participants.

ISBN 1 85717 148 3   October 1997   17pp   Price £5.00

Intermediate Care
A CONCEPTUAL FRAMEWORK AND REVIEW OF THE LITERATURE
Andrea Steiner

This is a report based on work that was undertaken on behalf of the King's Fund London Commission as part of its comprehensive review of London's health services. It highlights the range of intermediate care services, an appropriate taxonomy, the extent and quality of the literature and various policy issues.

ISBN 1 85717 152 7   August 1997   83pp   Price £5.00

Intermediate Care
APPROACHES TO EVALUATION
Andrea Steiner, Barbara Vaughan and Linda Hanford

This informative discussion paper focuses on an evaluation of intermediate care. It also provides a useful toolkit for those who wish to or need to systematically judge the merit of their intermediate care services.

ISBN 1 85717 222 1   July 1999   116pp   Price £5.00

Intermediate Care
SHIFTING THE MONEY
Andrea Steiner, Barbara Vaughan and Linda Hanford

This report explores the incentives and disincentives for funding intermediate care services and offers detailed examples of ways in which practitioners and managers have overcome the difficulties. It is useful for people who are interested in intermediate care and want to understand more about the issues involved in shifting the money.

ISBN 1 85717 264 7   February 1999   38pp   Price £5.99

Intermediate Care
THE SHAPE OF THE TEAM
Barbara Vaughan, Andrea Steiner and Linda Hanford

In this publication the intra- and inter- professional issues are examined in relation to shifting boundaries of responsibility among the professions and the continuum of health and social services. It also offers examples of ways in which people have 'made it work', and highlights implications at an organisational, policy and professional education level for consideration in the future.

ISBN 1 85717 269 8   February 1999   38pp   Price £5.99

 # Order form

Title	ISBN	Price	Quantity
Intermediate Care: Models in practice	1 85717 273 6	£10.99	
Intermediate Care: A discussion paper	1 85717 148 3	£5.00	
Intermediate Care: A conceptual framework and review of the literature	1 85717 152 7	£5.00	
Intermediate Care: Approaches to evaluation	1 85717 222 1	£5.00	
Intermediate Care: Shifting the money	1 85717 264 7	£5.99	
Intermediate Care: The shape of the team	1 85717 269 8	£5.99	

Total £ for titles

Postage and packing

Total order £

☐ I enclose a cheque for £_____
    made payable to King's Fund

☐ Please charge £_____ to my credit card account   (Please circle: Mastercard/Visa/Visa Delta/Switch)

Card No: _____

Expiry Date: _____

Issue No/Valid from date: _____

Title (Dr, Mr, Ms, Mrs, Miss): _____

First name: _____

Surname: _____

Job title: _____

Organisation: _____

Address: _____

_____

_____ Postcode: _____

Tel: _____ Fax:_____

E-mail: _____

Billing address (if different):

_____

_____

_____ Postcode: _____

POSTAGE AND PACKING – Please add **10%** of the total order value for **UK** (up to a maximum fee of £8.00). Please add **20%** if ordering from **Europe** (up to a maximum of £15.00). Please add **30%** if ordering from the **rest of the world** (up to a maximum of £30.00).

PLEASE NOTE – **Shortages must be reported** within ten days of delivery date. **We can invoice for orders of £35.00 and over** if a purchase order is supplied.

Please detach and send this order form to
KING'S FUND BOOKSHOP
11–13 CAVENDISH SQUARE, LONDON W1G 0AN

TEL **020 7307 2591**   FAX **020 7307 2801**
www.kingsfundbookshop.org.uk